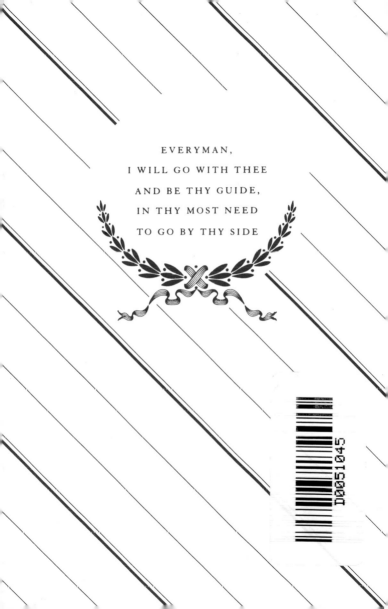

EVERYMAN,
I WILL GO WITH THEE
AND BE THY GUIDE,
IN THY MOST NEED
TO GO BY THY SIDE

EVERYMAN'S LIBRARY
POCKET POETS

Erotic Poems

Selected and edited by
Peter Washington

EVERYMAN'S LIBRARY

POCKET POETS

Alfred A. Knopf · New York · Toronto

THIS IS A BORZOI BOOK

PUBLISHED BY ALFRED A. KNOPF, INC.

This selection by Peter Washington first published in Everyman's
Library, 1994
Copyright © 1994 by David Campbell Publishers Ltd.
Fourth printing

A list of acknowledgments to copyright owners appears at the back of
this volume.

ISBN 0-679-43322-8
LC 94-2491

Library of Congress Cataloging-in-Publication Data
Erotic poems.
 p.   cm.—(Everyman's library pocket poems.)
Includes bibliographical references (p.).
ISBN 0-679-43322-8
1. Erotic poetry. I. Series.
PN6110.ES5E75   1994   94-2491
808.81'93538—dc20   CIP

Typography by Peter B. Willberg

Typeset in the UK by MS Filmsetting Limited, Frome, Somerset

Printed and bound in Germany by
Mohndruck Graphische Betriebe GmbH, Gütersloh

CONTENTS

6

9

FOREWORD

This anthology is a companion to the Everyman collection of *Love Poems*, distinguished from that volume by its preoccupation with the life of the body. That said, anyone looking for pornography here will be disappointed: on this occasion I have taken erotic to mean primarily sensuous and passionate. There *are* frank and even bawdy poems included, by Rochester among others; many of the items are witty and funny; others are tragic; but the emphasis is on Eros as the god of physical love, not the mere patron of genital conjunctions.

In *Love Poems* the poems were arranged according to categories. This time the anthology is founded on a chain of thematic associations which will soon be evident to any reader who follows the pages in sequence.

One piece of verse is repeated from *Love Poems*. Marlowe's translation of Ovid's fifth elegy has always seemed to me the supreme erotic poem in English after *The Eve of St Agnes*. I could not resist printing it again.

PETER WASHINGTON

EROTIC
POEMS

A second batch of verses by that naughty provincial
>   poet,
>   Naso, the chronicler of his own
Wanton frivolities; another of Love's commissions
>   (warning
>   To puritans: *This volume is not for you*).
I want my works to be read by the far-from-frigid
>   virgin
>   On fire for her sweetheart, by the boy
In love for the very first time. May some
>   fellow-sufferer,
>   Perusing my anatomy of desire,
See his own passion reflected there, cry in amazement:
>   'Who told this scribbler about my private affairs?'
One time, I recall, I got started on an inflated epic
>   About War in Heaven, with all
Those hundred-handed monsters, and Earth's fell
>   vengeance, and towering
>   Ossa piled on Olympus (plus Pelion too).
But while I was setting up Jove – stormclouds and
>   thunderbolts gathered
>   Ready to hand, a superb defensive barrage –
My mistress staged a lock-out. I dropped Jupiter and
>   his lightnings
>   That instant, didn't give him another thought.

15

Forgive me, good Lord, if I found your armoury
      useless –
   Her shut door ran to larger bolts
Then any *you* wielded. I went back to verses and
      compliments,
   My natural weapons. Soft words
Remove harsh door-chains. There's magic in poetry,
      its power
   Can pull down the bloody moon,
Turn back the sun, make serpents burst asunder
   Or rivers flow upstream.
Doors are no match for such spellbinding, the toughest
   Locks can be open-sesamed by its charms.
But epic's a dead loss for me. I'll get nowhere with
      swift-footed
   Achilles, or with either of Atreus' sons.
Old what's-his-name wasting twenty years on war and
      travel,
   Poor Hector dragged in the dust –
No good. But lavish fine words on some young girl's
      profile
   And sooner or later she'll tender herself as the fee,
An ample reward for your labours. So farewell, heroic
   Figures of legend – the *quid*
Pro quo you offer won't tempt me. A bevy of beauties
   All swooning over my love-songs – that's what *I*
      want.

NO PLATONIC LOVE

Tell me no more of minds embracing minds,
    And hearts exchang'd for hearts;
That spirits spirits meet, as winds do winds,
    And mix their subt'lest parts;
That two unbodied essences may kiss,
And then like Angels, twist and feel one Bliss.

I was that silly thing that once was wrought
    To practise this thin love;
I climb'd from sex to soul, from soul to thought;
    But thinking there to move,
Headlong I rolled from thought to soul, and then
From soul I lighted at the sex again.

As some strict down-looked men pretend to fast,
    Who yet in closets eat;
So lovers who profess they spirits taste,
    Feed yet on grosser meat;
I know they boast they souls to souls convey,
Howe'r they meet, the body is the way.

Come, I will undeceive thee, they that tread
   Those vain aerial ways,
Are like young heirs and alchemists misled
   To waste their wealth and days,
For searching thus to be for ever rich,
They only find a med'cine for the itch.

THE PARTNER

Between such animal and human heat
I find myself perplexed. What is desire? –
The impulse to make someone else complete?
That woman would set sodden straw on fire.
Was I the servant of a sovereign wish,
Or ladle rattling in an empty dish?

We played a measure with commingled feet:
The lively dead had taught us to be fond.
Who can embrace the body of his fate?
Light altered light along the living ground.
She kissed me close, and then did something else.
My marrow beat as wildly as my pulse.

I'd say it to my horse: we live beyond
Our outer skin. Who's whistling up my sleeve?
I see a heron prancing in his pond;
I know a dance the elephants believe.
The living all assemble! What's the cue? –
Do what the clumsy partner wants to do!

Things loll and loiter. Who condones the lost?
This joy outleaps the dog. Who cares? Who cares?
I gave her kisses back, and woke a ghost.
O what lewd music crept into our ears!
The body and the soul know how to play
In that dark world where gods have lost their way.

ADDRESS TO VENUS

Delight of Humane kind, and Gods above;
Parent of Rome; Propitious Queen of Love;
Whose vital pow'r, Air, Earth, and Sea supplies;
And breeds what e'r is born beneath the rowling Skies:
For every kind, by thy prolifique might,
Springs, and beholds the Regions of the light:
Thee, Goddess thee, the clouds and tempests fear,
And at thy pleasing presence disappear:
For thee the Land in fragrant Flow'rs is drest,
For thee the Ocean smiles, and smooths her wavy
     breast;
And Heav'n it self with more serene, and purer light
     is blest.
For when the rising Spring adorns the Mead,
And a new Scene of Nature stands display'd,
When teeming Budds, and chearful greens appear,
And Western gales unlock the lazy year,
The joyous Birds thy welcome first express,
Whose native Songs thy genial fire confess:
Then salvage Beasts bound o're their slighted food,
Strook with thy darts, and tempt the raging floud:
All Nature is thy Gift; Earth, Air, and Sea:
Of all that breaths, the various progeny,
Stung with delight, is goaded on by thee.
O're barren Mountains, o're the flow'ry Plain,

The leavy Forest, and the liquid Main
Extends thy uncontroul'd and boundless reign.
Through all the living Regions dost thou move,
And scatter'st, where thou goest, the kindly seeds
        of Love:
Since then the race of every living thing,
Obeys thy pow'r; since nothing new can spring
Without thy warmth, without thy influence bear,
Or beautiful, or lovesome can appear,
Be thou my ayd: My tuneful Song inspire,
And kindle with thy own productive fire;
While all thy Province Nature, I survey,
And sing to Memmius an immortal lay
Of Heav'n, and Earth, and every where thy wond'rous
        pow'r display.
To Memmius, under thy sweet influence born,
Whom thou with all thy gifts and graces dost adorn.
The rather, then assist my Muse and me,
Infusing Verses worthy him and thee.
Mean time on Land and Sea let barb'rous discord cease,
And lull the listning world in universal peace.
To thee, Mankind their soft repose must owe,
For thou alone that blessing canst bestow;
Because the brutal business of the War
Is manag'd by thy dreadful Servant's care:
Who oft retires from fighting fields, to prove
The pleasing pains of thy eternal Love:

And panting on thy breast, supinely lies,
While with thy heavenly form he feeds his famish'd
      eyes:
Sucks in with open lips, thy balmy breath,
By turns restor'd to life, and plung'd in pleasing death.
There while thy curling limbs about him move,
Involv'd and fetter'd in the links of Love,
When wishing all, he nothing can deny,
Thy Charms in that auspicious moment try;
With winning eloquence our peace implore,
And quiet to the weary World restore.

THE QUIET GLADES OF EDEN

All such proclivities are tabulated –
By trained pathologists, in detail too –
The obscener parts of speech compulsively
Shrouded in Classic Latin.

But though my pleasure in your feet and hair
Is ungainsayable, let me protest
(Dear love) I am no trichomaniac
And no foot-fetichist.

If it should please you, for your own best reasons,
To take and flog me with a rawhide whip,
I might (who knows?) surprisedly accept
This earnest of affection.

Nothing, agreed, is alien to love
When pure desire has overflowed its baulks;
But why must private sportiveness be viewed
Through public spectacles?

Enough, I will not claim a heart unfluttered
By these case-histories of aberrancy;
Nevertheless a long cool draught of water,
Or a long swim in the bay,

Serves to restore my wholesome appetite
For you and what we do at night together:
Which is no more than Adam did with Eve
In the quiet glades of Eden.

INVITATION TO THE VOYAGE

Imagine the magic
of living together
there, with all the time in the world
for loving each other,
for loving and dying
where even the landscape resembles you:
the suns dissolved
in overcast skies
have the same mysterious charm for me
as your wayward eyes
through crystal tears,
my sister, my child!

All is order there, and elegance,
pleasure, peace, and opulence.

Furniture gleaming
with the patina
of time itself in the room we would share;
the rarest flowers
mingling aromas
with amber's uncertain redolence;
encrusted ceilings
echoed in mirrors

and Eastern splendor on the walls –
   here all would whisper
   to the soul in secret
     her sweet mother tongue.

All is order there, and elegance,
   pleasure, peace, and opulence.

   On these still canals
   the freighters doze
fitfully: their mood is for roving,
   and only to flatter
   a lover's fancy
have they put in from the ends of the earth.
   By late afternoon
   the canals catch fire
as sunset glorifies the town;
   the world turns to gold
   as it falls asleep
     in a fervent light.

All is order there, and elegance,
   pleasure, peace, and opulence.

CHARLES BAUDELAIRE (1821–1867),   27
TRANS. RICHARD HOWARD

TO THE ETERNAL FEMININE

Figmental mannequin, Turk's-head for the trap,
Eternal Feminine! ... smooth out your fichus;
and when I say it's time, come to my lap,
show me, *chez* fallen angels, what they do.

Be worse than they, make us joy that goes awry;
with nimble feet prance up the arduous climb,
damn yourself, pure idol! laugh! sing! cry!
belov'd! and die for love ... in our spare time.

Marble girl! in rut! act crazy! ... have sport! ...
be pensive, mistress, my flesh! be virgin and whore ...
savage, holy and stupid, to find me a heart ...

Be female to the male, his Muse, and when
the poet bells: *Ame! Lame! Flamme!* ah, ther –
when he snores – come kiss your Conqueror!

28   TRISTAN CORBIÈRE (1845–1875),
    TRANS. C. F. MACINTYRE

TOUCH

My hands
Open the curtains of your being
Clothe you in a further nudity
Uncover the bodies of your body
My hands
Invent another body for your body

THE FEEL OF HANDS

The hands explore tentatively,
two small live entities whose shapes
I have to guess at. They touch me
all, with the light of fingertips

testing each surface of each thing
found, timid as kittens with it.
I connect them with amusing
hands I have shaken by daylight.

There is a sudden transition:
they plunge together in a full
formed single fury; they are grown
to cats, hunting without scruple;

they are expert but desperate.
I am in the dark. I wonder
when they grew up. It strikes me that
I do not know whose hands they are.

LOVER

Lover, secretly behind your smile
The words of love nakedly
Discover your breasts and your neck
And your hips and your eyelids
Discover every caress
So that the kisses in your eyes
Reveal entire the whole of you.

PAUL ÉLUARD (1895–1952),
TRANS. DEREK PARKER

THE HEAD OF HAIR

Ecstatic fleece that ripples to your nape
and reeks of negligence in every curl!
To people my dim cubicle tonight
with memories shrouded in that head of hair,
I'd have it flutter like a handkerchief!

For torpid Asia, torrid Africa
– the wilderness I thought a world away –
survive at the heart of this dark continent . . .
As other souls set sail to music, mine,
O my love! embarks on your redolent hair.

Take me, tousled current, to where men
as mighty as the trees they live among
submit like them to the sun's long tyranny;
ebony sea, you bear a brilliant dream
of sails and pennants, mariners and masks,

a harbor where my soul can slake its thirst
for color, sound and smell – where ships that glide
among the seas of golden silk throw wide
their yardarms to embrace a glorious sky
palpitating in eternal heat.

Drunk, and in love with drunkenness, I'll dive
into this ocean where the other lurks,
and solaced by these waves, my restlessness
will find a fruitful lethargy at last,
rocking forever at aromatic ease.

Blue hair, vault of shadows, be for me
the canopy of overarching sky;
here at the downy roots of every strand
I stupefy myself on the mingled scent
of musk and tar and coconut oil for hours ...

For hours? Forever! Into that splendid mane
let me braid rubies, ropes of pearls to bind
you indissolubly to my desire –
you the oasis where I dream, the gourd
from which I gulp the wine of memory.

CHARLES BAUDELAIRE (1821–1867),
TRANS. RICHARD HOWARD   33

IF THE FOREST OF HER HAIR

If the forest of her hair
Calls you to explore the land,
And her breasts, those mountains fair,
Tempt that mountaineer, your hand –
Stop! before it is too late:
Love, the brigand, lies in wait.

34   BHARTṚHARI (5TH CENTURY),
TRANS. JOHN BROUGH

ODE 105

Who shall interpret the Beloved's hair!
So subtly caught, and coiled, and garlanded –
That maze, that glittering net, that shining snare;
Men of the true faith, and alike untrue,
Trapped in that cunning ambush on her head,
Are captive there –
'T is but a little for such hair to do.

Thy beauty, love, is just a miracle,
An innocent gift that heaven gave to thee;
But ah! the uses thou hast put it to
Are downright sorcery.

Thy lips breathe out such healing that the time
Of Jesus is come back, and dead men rise;
So long thy locks, so strong, thy lovers climb,
Holding thereby, safe into Paradise.
On thy dark eyes a hundred blessings rain!
Though at each look indeed a lover dies,
Touching thy lips he comes to life again.

O wonderful astrology of love!
Thou science deep as ocean, and as high
As the last lonely light in yonder sky;
Hidden within the compass of thy lore
All folly of earth, all wisdom of heaven above,
Saving the knowledge how to love no more.

It was that draught out of the cup of love
That sent me to this other cup of wine;
HAFIZ, thy heart is captive – O beware
Lest thou thy soul lose too, and she entwine
Even thy faith in God in her long hair.

TWIN HILLS

Her hair dense as darkness,
Her face rich as the full moon:
Unbelievable contrasts
Couched in a seat of love.
Her eyes rival lotuses.
Seeing that girl today,
My eager heart
Is driven by desire.

Innocence and beauty
Adore her fair skin.
Her gold necklace
Is lightning
On the twin hills,
Her breasts. . . .

VIDYĀPATI (15TH CENTURY),
TRANS. DEBEN BHATTACHARYA

ROMAN ELEGIES IV

Two young brunettes in the library of the husband
of the more stunning one. Two youthful, tender
ovals hunch over pages: a Muse telling Fate the
    substance
of several things she tried to render.
The swish of old paper, of red crêpe de Chine.
    A humming
fan mixes violets, lavender, and carnations.
Braiding of hair: an elbow thrusts up its summit
accustomed to cumulus-thick formations.
Oh, a dark eye is obviously more fluent
in brown furniture, pomegranates, oak, shutters.
It's more keen, it's more cordial than a blue one;
to the blue one, though, nothing matters!
The blue one can always tell the owner
from the goods, especially before closing –
that is, time from living – and turn the latter over,
as tails strain to look at heads in tossing.

ODE 173

All the long night we talked of your long hair:
The hollow listening hours rolled darkly by,
The solemn world beneath the steady stars
To morning moved, sleep-walking up the sky;
Only in Shiraz in the realm of Fars
The dark night long kept open one bright eye –
'T was where we sat up talking of your hair.

Each one of us, though wounded and far spent,
With arrowed eyelash sticking in his heart,
Still longed to see that bow your eyebrow bent,
And speeding yet another poisoned dart.
For 't is so many days since we have heard
News of you, that our hearts grew faint with fear;
But now at last the East Wind brings us word:
Ah! blame him not – we had such need to hear.

Ere you were born love was not; through you fell
The bitter curse of beauty on the world –
Yes! it was all that hair upon your head;
Amid its crafty convolutions curled
All the dark arts of beauty lie in wait;
For even I, before I came to tread
That darkling way, among the saints did dwell,
And full of grace and safety was my state.

Open your tunic: I would lay my head
Upon your heart – ah! deep within your side
Silence and shelter sweet I ever found;
Else must I seek them in the grave instead.
When HAFIZ sleeps indeed beneath the ground,
Visit his grave – it was for you he died.

LAST DAWN

Your hair lost in the forest,
your feet touching mine.
Asleep you are bigger than the night,
but your dream fits within this room.
How much we are who are so little!
Outside a taxi passes
with its load of ghosts.
The river that runs by
                          is always
running back.

Will tomorrow be another day?

OCTAVIO PAZ (1914–   ),
TRANS. ELIOT WEINBERGER

ODES I.v

To whom now Pyrrha, art thou kind?
    To what heart-ravisht Lover
Dost thou thy golden Locks unbind,
    Thy hidden sweets discover,
    And with large bounty open set
All the bright stores of the rich Cabinet?

Ah simple Youth, how oft will he
    Of thy chang'd Faith complain?
And his own Fortunes find to be
    So airy and so vain,
    Of so Chamelion-like an hew,
That still their colour changes with it too?

How oft, alas, will he admire
    The blackness of the Skies?
Trembling to hear the Winds sound higher
    And see the Billows rise;
    Poor unexperienc'd He
Who ne'r, alas, before had been at Sea!

He enjoys thy calmy Sun-shine now,
    And no breath stirring hears;
In the clear Heaven of thy brow
    No smallest Cloud appears.
    He sees thee gentle, fair, and gay,
And trusts the faithless April of thy May.

Unhappy, thrice unhappy He,
    T' whom Thou untry'd dost shine!
But there's no danger now for Me,
    Since o'r Loretto's Shrine
    In witness of the Shipwrack past
My consecrated Vessel hangs at last.

HORACE (65–8 BC),
TRANS. JAMES DUNCOMBE

THREE POEMS

1

On sunny days there in the shade
Beneath the trees reclined a maid
Who lifted up her dress (she said)
To keep the moonbeams off her head.

2

A hundred times they kiss, and then
    A thousand times embrace,
And stop only to start again;
There's no tautology in such a case.

3

He held her face, and would not let her go:
She tried to say, 'Oh no! No, no! Oh no,
No, no!' But through the kiss no sound would come
Except *'Hmm-hmm-hmm hm hm hmm hm hmmmm!*

BHARTṚHARI (5TH CENTURY),
TRANS. JOHN BROUGH

ANTONY AND CLEOPATRA

Together they stood watching on the terrace
As Egypt fell asleep under a stifling heaven
And the Nile rolled its fatness down to cleave
Its own black delta, to Sais or to Bubastis.

The Roman soldier, now a prisoner caught
Nursing a sleepy child, under the weight of his cuirass
Feels the luxurious body he embraces
Bend and give way on his triumphant heart.

Turning her face, pale in brown hair, to meet
This man half-drunk on her invincible scents,
Now she holds up her mouth and her clear eyes;

Bent over her the Imperator sees
In her wide pupils starred with golden points
An immeasurable sea with ships in flight.

JOSÉ-MARIA DE HEREDIA (1842–1905),   45
TRANS. ALISTAIR ELLIOT

BREASTS

They are firm, and you are tender,
Full and round, though you are slender:
Bold your breasts, while you are shy
– Since so near your heart they lie.

BHARTṚHARI, (5TH CENTURY)
TRANS. JOHN BROUGH

He marvelled at her breasts, and when he'd seen them
He shook his head, to disengage his gaze
Trapped in between them.

AMARU (5TH CENTURY),
TRANS. JOHN BROUGH

SEVEN STROPHES

I was but what you'd brush
with your palm, what your leaning
brow would hunch to in evening's
raven-black hush.

I was but what your gaze
in that dark could distinguish:
a dim shape to begin with,
later – features, a face.

It was you, on my right,
on my left, with your heated
sighs, who molded my helix,
whispering at my side.

It was you by that black
window's trembling tulle pattern
who laid in my raw cavern
a voice calling you back.

I was practically blind.
You, appearing, then hiding,
gave me my sight and heightened
it. Thus some leave behind

a trace. Thus they make worlds.
Thus, having done so, at random
wastefully they abandon
their work to its whirls.

Thus, prey to speeds
of light, heat, cold, or darkness,
a sphere in space without markers
spins and spins.

JOSEPH BRODSKY (1940–   ),
TRANS. PAUL GRAVES

GIFT OF SIGHT

I had long known the diverse tastes of the wood,
Each leaf, each bark, rank earth from every hollow;
Knew the smells of bird's breath and of bat's wing;
Yet sight I lacked: until you stole upon me,
Touching my eyelids with light finger-tips.
The trees blazed out, their colours whirled together,
Nor ever before had I been aware of sky.

ROBERT GRAVES (1895–1985)   49

THE VOICE

One feather is a bird,
I claim; one tree, a wood;
In her low voice I heard
More than a mortal should;
And so I stood apart,
Hidden in my own heart.

And yet I roamed out where
Those notes went, like the bird,
Whose thin song hung in air,
Diminished, yet still heard:
I lived with open sound,
Aloft, and on the ground.

That ghost was my own choice,
The shy cerulean bird;
It sang with her true voice,
And it was I who heard
A slight voice reply;
I heard; and only I.

Desire exults the ear:
Bird, girl, and ghostly tree,
The earth, the solid air –
Their slow song sang in me;
The long noon pulsed away,
Like any summer day.

ROSY EAR

I thought
but I know her so well
we have been living together so many years

I know
her bird-like head
white arms
and belly

until one time
on a winter evening
she sat down beside me
and in the lamplight
falling from behind us
I saw a rosy ear

a comic petal of skin
a conch with living blood
inside it

I didn't say anything then –

it would be good to write
a poem about a rosy ear
but not so that people would say
what a subject he chose
he's trying to be eccentric

so that nobody even would smile
so that they would understand that I proclaim
a mystery

I didn't say anything then
but that night when we were in bed together
delicately I essayed
the exotic taste
of a rosy ear

ZBIGNIEW HERBERT (1924–   ),
TRANS. CZESLAW MILOSZ

ZOO KEEPER'S WIFE

I can stay awake all night, if need be –
Cold as an eel, without eyelids.
Like a dead lake the dark envelops me,
Blueblack, a spectacular plum fruit.
No airbubbles start from my heart, I am lungless
And ugly, my belly a silk stocking
Where the heads and tails of my sisters decompose.
Look, they are melting like coins in the powerful
    juices –

The spidery jaws, the spine bones bared for a moment
Like the white lines on a blueprint.
Should I stir, I think this pink and purple plastic
Guts bag would clack like a child's rattle,
Old grievances jostling each other, so many loose
    teeth.
But what do you know about that
My fat pork, my marrowy sweetheart,
    face-to-the-wall?
Some things of this world are indigestible.

You wooed me with the wolf-headed fruit bats
Hanging from their scorched hooks in the moist
Fug of the Small Mammal House.
The armadillo dozed in his sandbin

Obscene and bald as a pig, the white mice
Multiplied to infinity like angels on a pinhead
Out of sheer boredom. Tangled in the sweat-wet
    sheets
I remembered the bloodied chicks and the quartered
    rabbits.

You checked the diet charts and took me to play
With the boa constrictor in the Fellows' Garden.
I pretended I was the Tree of Knowledge.
I entered your bible, I boarded your ark
With the sacred baboon in his wig and wax ears
And the bear-furred, bird-eating spider
Clambering round its glass box like an eight-fingered
    hand.
I can't get it out of my mind

How our courtship lit the tindery cages –
Your two-horned rhinoceros opened a mouth
Dirty as a bootsole and big as a hospital sink
For my cube of sugar: its bog breath
Gloved my arm to the elbow.
The snails blew kisses like black apples.
Nightly now I flog apes owls bears sheep
Over their iron stile. And still don't sleep.

SYLVIA PLATH (1932–1963)   55

MANY THINK QUINTIA'S BEAUTIFUL

Many think Quintia's beautiful. She's tall
And well-proportioned and her skin is white.
I grant her these good points, but I won't call
Her 'beautiful'. She has one fatal fault –
No sex-appeal: there's not a grain of salt
In that big dish to stir the appetite.
Lesbia *is* beautiful – not only blessed
With better looks than other girls, but dressed
In the mystery she's stolen from the rest.

From THE RAPE OF THE LOCK

Sol through white curtains shot a tim'rous ray,
And oped those eyes that must eclipse the day:
Now lapdogs gave themselves the rousing shake,
And sleepless lovers, just at twelve, awake:
Thrice rung the bell, the slipper knocked the ground,
And the pressed watch returned a silver sound.
Belinda still her downy pillow pressed,
Her guardian sylph prolonged the balmy rest.
  And now, unveiled, the toilet stands displayed,
Each silver vase in mystic order laid.
First, robed in white, the nymph intent adores,
With head uncovered, the cosmetic powers.
A heav'nly image in the glass appears,
To that she bends, to that her eyes she rears;
Th'inferior priestess, at her altar's side,
Trembling, begins the sacred rites of pride.
Unnumbered treasures ope at once, and here
The various offerings of the world appear;
From each she nicely culls with curious toil,
And decks the goddess with the glittering spoil.
This casket India's glowing gems unlocks,
And all Arabia breathes from yonder box.
The tortoise here and elephant unite,
Transformed to combs, the speckled, and the white.
Here files of pins extend their shining rows,

Puffs, powders, patches, Bibles, billet-doux.
Now awful beauty puts on all its arms;
The fair each moment rises in her charms,
Repairs her smiles, awakens every grace,
And calls forth all the wonders of her face;
Sees by degrees a purer blush arise,
And keener lightnings quicken in her eyes.
The busy sylphs surround their darling care,
These set the head, and those divide the hair,
Some fold the sleeve, while others plait the gown;
And Betty's praised for labours not her own.

THE WOMAN UNDERNEATH

On reflection, it all came down to nylon –
stockings, bras, pants.
Of course, there were the other things –
swing of buttocks, flap of breasts,

a whole shape of arc and indent.
But, somehow, it was the synthetics,
hitched nylon, an erotic mechanics,
that set us light years apart.

What did we have when we undressed?
Socks. Jockeys. A string vest.
But when they stepped out
of shoes, blouse, and skirt –

voilà! the French maid: that circumflex
of taut stocking-band; knickers
sheeny as a courtesan's; the stripper's

unhooking acrobatics; and the Lautrec
girl stooping as puckered hose slithers.
They held us in a man-made scissors.

ROBERT MAÎTRE (1944–   )   59

DELIGHT IN DISORDER

A sweet disorder in the dress
Kindles in clothes a wantonness:
A lawn about the shoulders thrown
Into a fine distraction,
An erring lace, which here and there
Enthralls the crimson stomacher,
A cuff neglectful, and thereby
Ribbands to flow confusedly,
A winning wave (deserving note)
In the tempestuous petticoat,
A careless shoe-string, in whose tie
I see a wild civility,
Do more bewitch me, than when art
Is too precise in every part.

From LOVE IN THE VALLEY

This I may know: her dressing and undressing
   Such a change of light shows as when the skies in
      sport
Shift from cloud to moonlight; or edging over thunder
   Slips a ray of sun; or sweeping into port
White sails furl; or on the ocean borders
   White sails lean along the waves leaping green.
Visions of her shower before me, but from eyesight
   Guarded she would be like the sun were she seen.

*   *   *   *   *   *

O the golden sheaf, the rustling treasure-armful!
   O the nutbrown tresses nodding interlaced!
O the treasure-tresses one another over
   Nodding! O the girdle slack about the waist!
Slain are the poppies that shot their random scarlet,
   Quick amid the wheatears: wound about the waist,
Gathered, see these brides of Earth one blush of
      ripeness!
   O the nutbrown tresses nodding interlaced!

ODE 147

Beauty alone will not account for her;
No single attribute her charm explains;
Though each be named, beyond it glimmers she,
Strangely distinct, mysteriously fair:
Hers this, this hers, and this – yet she remains.
Wonderful are her locks – she is not there;
Her body a spirit is – it is not she;
Her waist the compass of a silken thread;
Her mouth a ruby – but it is not she:
Say all of her, yet hast thou nothing said.
Surely the beauty of houri or of fay
A fashion of beauty is – but to my eye
Her way of beauty is beauty's only way

Unto this spring, sweet rose, pray draw anigh;
Sweet water 't is – my tears – to water thee.

Thine eye, ah! what an arrow! thine eyebrow,
How strong a bow! and what an archer thou!
Ah! what a target hast thou made of me.

Love's secret verily no one man knows,
Though each in lore of loving deems him wise;
Love's like a meadow all aflower with spring,
But in the shadow autumn waiting lies,
And the wise bird is half afraid to sing –
A vanished song unto a vanished rose.

HAFIZ, a power strange to touch the heart
Of late hath stolen subtly in thy song,
Through thy firm reed unwonted pathos blows;
Her praise it is, and no new touch of art,
That gives this grace of tears unto thy song.

HAFIZ (*d. c.* 1390),   63
TRANS. RICHARD LE GALLIENNE

TO WHAT SERVES MORTAL BEAUTY?

To what serves mortal beauty – dangerous; does set danc-
ing blood – the O-seal-that-so feature, flung prouder form
Than Purcell tune lets tread to? See: it does this: keeps
    warm
Men's wits to the things that are; what good means –
    where a glance
Master more may than gaze, gaze out of countenance.
Those lovely lads once, wet-fresh windfalls of war's storm,
How then should Gregory, a father, have gleanèd else
    from swarm-
èd Rome? But God to a nation dealt that day's dear chance.
  To man, that needs would worship block or barren stone,
Our law says: Love what are love's worthiest, were all known
World's loveliest – men's selves. Self flashes off frame and fac
What do then? how meet beauty? Merely meet it; own,
Home at heart, heaven's sweet gift; then leave, let that alone.
Yea, wish that though, wish all, God's better beauty, grace.

From EPIPSYCHIDION

She met me, Stranger, upon life's rough way,
And lured me towards sweet Death; as Night by Day,
Winter by Spring, or Sorrow by swift Hope,
Led into light, life, peace. An antelope,
In the suspended impulse of its lightness,
Were less aethereally light: the brightness
Of her divinest presence trembles through
Her limbs, as underneath a cloud of dew
Embodied in the windless Heaven of June
Amid the splendour-wingèd stars, the Moon
Burns, inextinguishably beautiful:
And from her lips, as from a hyacinth full
Of honey-dew, a liquid murmur drops,
Killing the sense with passion; sweet as stops
Of planetary music heard in trance.
In her mild lights the starry spirits dance,
The sun-beams of those wells which ever leap
Under the lightnings of the soul – too deep
For the brief fathom-line of thought or sense.
The glory of her being, issuing thence,
Stains the dead, blank, cold air with a warm shade
Of unentangled intermixture, made
By Love, of light and motion: one intense
Diffusion, one serene Omnipresence,
Whose flowing outlines mingled in their flowing,

Around her cheeks and utmost fingers glowing
With the unintermitted blood, which there
Quivers, (as in a fleece of snow-like air
The crimson pulse of living morning quiver,)
Continuously prolonged, and ending never,
Till they are lost, and in that Beauty furled
Which penetrates and clasps and fills the world;
Scarce visible from extreme loveliness.
Warm fragrance seems to fall from her light dress,
And her loose hair; and where some heavy tress
The air of her own speed has disentwined,
The sweetness seems to satiate the faint wind;
And in the soul a wild odour is felt,
Beyond the sense, like fiery dews that melt
Into the bosom of a frozen bud. —
See where she stands! a mortal shape indued
With love and life and light and deity,
And motion which may change but cannot die;
An image of some bright Eternity;
A shadow of some golden dream; a Splendour
Leaving the third sphere pilotless; a tender
Reflection of the eternal Moon of Love
Under whose motions life's dull billows move;
A Metaphor of Spring and Youth and Morning;
A Vision like incarnate April, warning,
With smiles and tears, Frost the Anatomy
Into his summer grave.

NEW LOVE

Style of the new moon, stirrings of new love,
Scratches of nails scarring her firm breasts.
At times she eyes them and at times she shields,
As poor hands cover treasure dear as life.
For the first time she knew the act of love.
The joys of dalliance fill her thoughts,
Wrapping her round with shudderings of delight.
Safe from the eyes of vicious friends,
She holds a gem as mirror to her face,
Lowers her brow that none can see
And then with tender care
Studies the love-bites on her lower lip.

VIDYĀPATI (15TH CENTURY),
TRANS. DEBEN BHATTACHARYA

SERENATA

The night soaks itself
along the shore of the river
and in Lolita's breasts
the branches die of love.

The branches die of love.

Naked the night sings
above the bridges of March.
Lolita bathes her body
with salt water and roses.

The branches die of love.

The night of anise and silver
shines over the rooftops.
Silver of streams and mirrors.
Anise of your white thighs.

The branches die of love.

FEDERICO GARCÍA LORCA (1898–1936),
TRANS. DEREK PARKER

EXOTIC SCENT

On a warm autumn evening, if I shut both eyes
And breathe the smell of heat from your warm breast,
I see unfolding a long happy coast
That endless sun has burnt into a daze;

An island state of sloth, where nature grows
The strangest trees, and fruits of delicate taste;
Where men are lean and strong, and women rest
Their eyes on one with startling openness.

Following your smell toward this charming zone,
I see a harbour full of masts and sails
Still shaken from the ocean waves and winds,

And then the scent of verdant tamarinds
Comes wafting to my heart and swells my nostrils,
Mixed with the shanties of the deep-sea men.

CHARLES BAUDELAIRE (1821 1867),
TRANS. ALISTAIR ELLIOT

AH WHEN YOU DRIFT

Ah when you drift hover before you kiss
More my mouth yours now, lips grow more to mine
Teeth click, suddenly your tongue like a mulled wine
Slides fire, – I wonder what the point of life is.
Do, down this night when I adore you, Lise,
So I forsake the blest assistant shine
Of deep-laid maps I made for summits, swine-
enchanted lover, loafing in the abyss?

Loaf hardly, while my nerves dance, while the gale
Moans like your hair down here. But I lie still,
Strengthless and smiling under a maenad rule.
Whose limbs worked once, whose imagination's grail
Many or some would nourish, must now I fill
My strength with desire, my cup with your tongue,
  no more Melpomene's, but Erato's fool? . . .

WHEN HIS MOUTH FACED MY MOUTII

When his mouth faced my mouth, I turned aside
And steadfastly gazed only at the ground;
I stopped my ears, when at each coaxing word
They tingled more; I used both hands to hide
My blushing, sweating cheeks. Indeed, I tried.
But oh, what could I do, then, when I found
My bodice splitting of its own accord?

AMARU (5TH CENTURY),
TRANS. JOHN BROUGH

THE MAID'S THOUGHT

Why listen, even the water is sobbing for something.
The west wind is dead, the waves
Forget to hate the cliff, in the upland canyons
Whole hillsides burst aglow
With golden broom. Dear how it rained last month,
And every pool was rimmed
With sulphury pollen dust of the wakening pines.
Now tall and slender suddenly
The stalks of purple iris blaze by the brooks,
The penciled ones on the hill:
This deerweed shivers with gold, the white
    globe-tulips
Blow out their silky bubbles,
But in the next glen bronze-bells nod, the does
Scalded by some hot longing
Can hardly set their pointed hoofs to expect
Love but they crush a flower;
Shells pair on the rock, birds mate, the moths fly
    double.
O it is time for us now
Mouth kindling mouth to entangle our maiden bodies
To make that burning flower.

KISSES LOATHSOME

I abhor the slimie kisse,
(Which to me most loathsome is.)
Those lips please me which are plac't
Close, but not too strictly lac't:
Yeilding I wo'd have them; yet
Not a wimbling Tongue admit:
What sho'd poking-sticks make there,
When the ruffe is set elsewhere?

ROBERT HERRICK (1591–1674)

ARIA

'Kiss me there where pride is glistening,
Kiss me where I am round or ripened fruit,
Kiss me wherever however whenever
   I am supple and flare and bare,
Let the belle be rung as long as I am young,
   let ring and fly like a great bronze wing
Until I am shaken from blossom to root.'

'– I'll kiss you wherever you think you are poor,
Wherever you shudder, feeling tiny or skinny, striped
      or barred,
Feeling you are bloodless, cheerless, chapless or
      marred
               Until, until
            Your gaze has been stilled
Until you are shamed again no more!
I'll kiss you until your body and soul
   – the mind in the body being fulfilled –
Suspend their dread and civil war.'

From DON JUAN, CANTO II

And thus they wandered forth, and hand in hand,
    Over the shining pebbles and the shells,
Glided along the smooth and hardened sand,
    And in the worn and wild receptacles
Worked by the storms, yet worked as it were planned,
    In hollow halls, with sparry roofs and cells,
They turned to rest; and, each clasped by an arm,
Yielded to the deep twilight's purple charm.

They looked up to the sky, whose floating glow
    Spread like a rosy ocean, vast and bright;
They gazed upon the glittering sea below,
    Whence the broad moon rose circling into sight;
They heard the waves splash, and the wind so low,
    And saw each other's dark eyes darting light
Into each other – and, beholding this,
Their lips drew near, and clung into a kiss;

A long, long kiss, a kiss of youth, and love,
    And beauty, all concentrating like rays
Into one focus, kindled from above;
    Such kisses as belong to early days,
Where heart, and soul, and sense, in concert move,
    And the blood's lava, and the pulse a blaze,
Each kiss a heart-quake – for a kiss's strength,
I think, it must be reckoned by its length.

By length, I mean duration; theirs endured
    Heaven knows how long – no doubt they never
        reckoned;
And if they had, they could not have secured
    The sum of their sensations to a second:
They had not spoken; but they felt allured,
    As if their souls and lips each other beckoned,
Which, being joined, like swarming bees they clung –
Their hearts the flowers from whence the honey
        sprung.

They were alone, but not alone as they
    Who shut in chambers think it loneliness;
The silent ocean, and the starlit bay,
    The twilight glow, which momently grew less,
The voiceless sands, and dropping caves, that lay
    Around them, made them to each other press,
As if there were no life beneath the sky
Save theirs, and that their life could never die.

They feared no eyes nor ears on that lone beach,
    They felt no terrors from the night; they were
All in all to each other; though their speech
    Was broken words, they *thought* a language there –
And all the burning tongues the passions teach
    Found in one sigh the best interpreter
Of nature's oracle – first love – that all
Which Eve has left her daughters since her fall.

THE SENSUALISTS

'There is no place to turn,' she said,
     'You have me pinned so close;
My hair's all tangled on your head,
     My back is just one bruise;
I feel we're breathing with the dead;
     O angel, let me loose!'

And she was right, for there beside
     The gin and cigarettes,
A woman stood, pure as a bride,
     Affrighted from her wits,
And breathing hard, as that man rode
     Between those lovely tits.

'My shoulder's bitten from your teeth;
  What's that peculiar smell?
No matter which one is beneath,
  Each is an animal,' –
The ghostly figure sucked its breath,
  And shuddered toward the wall;
Wrapped in the tattered robe of death,
  It tiptoed down the hall.

'The bed itself begins to quake,
  I hate this sensual pen;
My neck, if not my heart, will break
  If we do this again,' –
Then each fell back, limp as a sack,
  Into the world of men.

DRAFT FOR A CONTEMPORARY
LOVE POEM

For surely whiteness
is best described through greyness
bird through stone
sunflowers
in December

in the past love poems
described flesh
described this and that
eyelashes for instance

surely redness
should be described
through greyness sun through rain
poppies in November
lips at night

the most telling
description of bread
is one of hunger
it includes
the damp porous centre
the warm interior
sunflowers at night
breasts belly thighs of Cybele

a spring-like
transparent description
of water
is the description of thirst
of ashes
desert
it conjures up a mirage
clouds and trees enter
the mirror

Hunger deprivation
absence
of flesh
is the description of love
the contemporary love poem

TADEUSZ RÓŻEWICZ (1921–   ),   81
TRANS. ADAM CZERNIAWSKI

ONE NIGHT

The room was poor and squalid,
hidden above the dubious tavern.
From the window you could see the alley
filthy and narrow. From below
came the voices of some workmen
playing cards and carousing.

And there on the much-used, lowly bed
I had the body of love, I had the lips,
the voluptuous and rosy lips of ecstasy –
rosy lips of such ecstasy, that even now
as I write, after so many years!
in my solitary house, I am drunk again.

C. P. CAVAFY (1863–1933),
TRANS. RAE DALVEN

MY DOWNFALL

My downfall: those pink articulate lips
Divinely flavoured portals to a mouth
Where soul dissolves . . . eyes darting
Beneath black brows, snares for the heart,
And the milk-white breasts, well shaped,
The twin rosebuds, fair beyond other flowers.

To itemize thus – is this to cast dogs a bone?
The poet's pen – secret as reeds of Midas?

DIOSKORIDES (3RD CENTURY BC),
TRANS. PETER WHIGHAM

TO THE STATE OF LOVE OR THE SENSES' FESTIVAL

I saw a vision yesternight,
Enough to sate a Seeker's sight;
I wished myself a Shaker there,
And her quick pants my trembling sphere.
It was a she so glittering bright,
You'd think her soul an Adamite;
A person of so rare a frame,
Her body might be lined with' same.
Beauty's chiefest maid of honour,
You may break Lent with looking on her.
  Not the fair Abbess of the skies,
  With all her nunnery of eyes,
  Can show me such a glorious prize!

And yet, because 'tis more renown
To make a shadow shine, she's brown;
A brown for which Heaven would disband
The galaxy, and stars be tanned;
Brown by reflection as her eye
Deals out the summer's livery.
Old dormant windows must confess
Her beams; their glimmering spectacles,
Struck with the splendour of her face,
Do th' office of a burning-glass.
    Now where such radiant lights have shown,
    No wonder if her cheeks be grown
    Sunburned, with lustre of her own.

My sight took pay, but (thank my charms!)
I now impale her in mine arms;
(Love's compasses confining you,
Good angels, to a circle too.)
Is not the universe strait-laced
When I can clasp it in the waist?
My amorous folds about thee hurled,
With Drake I girdle in the world;
I hoop the firmament, and make
This, my embrace, the zodiac.
    How would thy centre take my sense
    When admiration doth commence
    At the extreme circumference?

Now to the melting kiss that sips
The jellied philtre of her lips;
So sweet there is no tongue can praise't
Till transubstantiate with a taste.
Inspired like Mahomet from above
By th' billing of my heavenly dove,
Love prints his signets in her smacks,
Those ruddy drops of squeezing wax,
Which, wheresoever she imparts,
They're privy seal to take up hearts.
    Our mouths encountering at the sport,
    My slippery soul had quit the fort,
    But that she stopped the sally-port.

Next to these sweets, her lips dispense
(As twin conserves of eloquence)
The sweet perfume her breath affords,
Incorporating with her words.
No rosary this vot'ress needs –
Her very syllables are beads;
No sooner 'twixt those rubies born,
But jewels are in ear-rings worn.
With what delight her speech doth enter;
It is a kiss o' th' second venter.
    And I dissolve at what I hear,
    As if another Rosamond were
    Couched in the labyrinth of my ear.

Yet that's but a preludious bliss,
Two souls pickeering in a kiss.
Embraces do but draw the line,
'Tis storming that must take her in.
When bodies join and victory hovers
'Twixt the equal fluttering lovers,
This is the game; make stakes, my dear!
Hark, how the sprightly chanticleer
(That Baron Tell-clock of the night)
Sounds boutesel to Cupid's knight.
   Then have at all, the pass is got,
   For coming off, oh, name it not!
   Who would not die upon the spot?

ELEGY 5

In summer's heat and mid-time of the day
To rest my limbs upon a bed I lay,
One window shut, the other open stood,
Which gave such light, as twinkles in a wood,
Like twilight glimpse at setting of the sun,
Or night being past, and yet not day begun.
Such light to shamefast maidens must be shown,
Where they must sport, and seem to be unknown.
Then came Corinna in a long loose gown,
Her white neck hid with tresses hanging down:
Resembling fair Semiramis going to bed
Or Layis of a thousand wooers sped.
I snatched her gown, being thin, the harm was small,
Yet strived she to be covered there withal.
And striving thus as one that would be cast,
Betrayed herself, and yielded at the last.
Stark naked as she stood before mine eye,
Not one wen in her body could I spy.
What arms and shoulders did I touch and see,
How apt her breasts were to be pressed by me?
How smooth a belly under her waist saw I?
How large a leg, and what a lusty thigh?
To leave the rest, all liked me passing well,
I clinged her naked body, down she fell,
Judge you the rest, being tired she bade me kiss,
Jove send me more such afternoons as this.

88   OVID (43 BC–18 AD),
        TRANS. CHRISTOPHER MARLOWE

From L'APRÈS-MIDI D'UN FAUNE

Between the reeds I saw their bodies gleam
Who cool no mortal fever in the stream
Crying to the woods the rage of their desires
And their bright hair went down in jeweled fire
Where crystal broke and dazzled shudderingly.
I check my swift pursuit: for see where lie,
Bruised, being twins in love, my languor sweet,
Two sleeping girls, clasped at my very feet.
I seize and run with them, nor part the pair,
Breaking this covert of frail petals, where
Roses drink scent of the sun and our light play
'Mid tumbled flowers shall match the death of day.
I love that virginal fury – ah, the wild
Thrill when a maiden body shrinks, defiled,
Shuddering like arctic light, from lips that sear
Its nakedness . . . the flesh in secret fear!
Contagiously through my linked pair it flies
Where innocence in either, struggling, dies,
Wet with fond tears or some less piteous dew.
Gay in the conquest of these fears, I grew
So rash that I must needs the sheaf divide
Of ruffled kisses heaven itself had tied.
For as I leaned to stifle in the hair
Of one my passionate laughter (taking care
With a stretched finger, that her innocence

Might stain with her companion's kindling sense
To touch the younger little one, who lay
Child-like, unblushing) my ungrateful prey
Slips from me, freed by passion's sudden death
Nor heeds the frenzy of my sobbing breath.
Let it pass! others of their hair shall twist
A rope to drag me to those joys I missed.
See how the ripe pomegranates bursting red
To quench the thirst of the mumbling bees have bled;
So too our blood, kindled by some chance fire,
Flows for the swarming legions of desire.
At evening, when the woodland green turns gold
And ashen gray, 'mid the quenched leaves, behold!
Red Etna glows, by Venus visited,
Walking the lava with her snowy tread
Whene'er the flames in thunderous slumber die.
I hold the goddess!

          Ah, sure penalty!

But the unthinking soul and body swoon
At last beneath the heavy hush of noon.
Forgetful let me lie where summer's drouth
Sifts fine the sand and then with gaping mouth
Dream planet-struck by the grape's round wine-red
    star.

Nymphs, I shall see the shade that now you are.

90   STEPHANE MALLARMÉ (1842–1898),
      TRANS. ALDOUS HUXLEY

ELEGY XIX (A KISS)

Without a soul, a mind, a breath, or pulse,
I held no strings of arteries, veins or muscles –
All had untied themselves in love's hot fight.
A veil of darkness bandaged up my sight,
My ears had started ringing, my tongue dried
And stuck with heat to some cave-roof inside,
My arms half-fallen-off ensnared your throat,
I fainted, lungs too weak to vent a note,
That gloomy kingdom swam before my eyes
Which never knows the heavenly joy of skies,
I saw the kingdom that King Pluto chose,
And worm-holes in the boat old Charon rows.
In short, half-dead, I felt your lungs inflate
And with a warmly sighing breath translate
Into my mouth a kiss, soon broken up among
Sweet puffs of laughter and your darting lizard tongue –
A kiss that fed my soul and made me live,
A sweet kind flame, moist and restorative,
That banished death and darkness from my eyelids
And made the boat of the old man who guides
The souls of lovers to the shore of love,
Leave without taking mine – too ill to move.
So I was cured by the spirit of a kiss.

Let's stop appeasing (at a cost like this)
My Cyprian heat, dear heart, especially days
When Sol rolls underneath the Dog to blaze
And, throwing rays of sunstroke from his torch,
Burns up our blood and makes the summer scorch.
Let's make truce now, save up vitality,
For fear (ill-armed in our philosophy)
We feel too soon – or afterwards, at leisure –
Anguish is always there, next door to pleasure.

THE DREAM

1

I met her as a blossom on a stem
Before she ever breathed, and in that dream
The mind remembers from a deeper sleep:
Eye learned from eye, cold lip from sensual lip.
My dream divided on a point of fire;
Light hardened on the water where we were;
A bird sang low; the moonlight sifted in;
The water rippled, and she rippled on.

2

She came toward me in the flowing air,
A shape of change, encirled by its fire.
I watched her there, between me and the moon;
The bushes and the stones danced on and on;
I touched her shadow when the light delayed;
I turned my face away, and yet she stayed.
A bird sang from the center of a tree;
She loved the wind because the wind loved me.

3

Love is not love until love's vulnerable.
She slowed to sigh, in that long interval.
A small bird flew in circles where we stood;
The deer came down, out of the dappled wood.
All who remember, doubt. Who calls that strange?
I tossed a stone, and listened to its plunge.
She knew the grammar of least motion, she
Lent me one virtue, and I live thereby.

4

She held her body steady in the wind;
Our shadows met, and slowly swung around;
She turned the field into a glittering sea;
I played in flame and water like a boy
And I swayed out beyond the white seafoam;
Like a wet log, I sang within a flame.
In that last while, eternity's confine,
I came to love, I came into my own.

THE VINE

I dreamed this mortal part of mine
Was metamorphosed to a vine;
Which crawling one and every way,
Enthralled my dainty Lucia.
Me thought, her long small legs and thighs
I with my tendrils did surprise;
Her belly, buttocks, and her waist
By now soft nervelets were embraced:
About her head I writhing hung,
And with rich clusters (hid among
The leaves) her temples I behung
So that my Lucia seemed to me
Young Bacchus ravished by his tree.
My curls about her neck did crawl,
And arms and hands they did enthral:
So that she could not freely stir,
(All parts there made one prisoner).
But when I crept with leaves to hide
Those parts, which maids keep unespied,
Such fleeting pleasures there I took,
That with the fancy I awoke;
And found (Ah me!) this flesh of mine
More like a stock, than like a vine.

ROBERT HERRICK (1591–1674)

PROOF

Her skin, saffron toasted in the sun,
eyes darting like a gazelle.

– That god who made her, how could he
have left her alone? Was he blind?

– This wonder is not the result of blindness:
she is a woman, and a sinuous vine.

The Buddha's doctrine thus is proven:
nothing in this world was created.

ELEGIES, I.iv

Yield prompt compliance to the maid's desires;
A prompt compliance fans the lover's fires:
Go pleas'd where'er she goes, tho' long the way,
Tho' the fierce Dog-star dart his sultry ray;
Tho' painted Iris gird the bluish sky,
And sure portends, that rattling storms are nigh:
Or, if the fair-one pant for sylvan fame,
Gay drag the meshes, and provoke the game:
Nay, should she choose to risk the driving gale;
Or steer, or row, or agile hand the sail:
No toil, tho' weak, tho' fearful, thou forbear;
No toils should tire you, and no dangers scare:
Occasion smiles, then snatch an ardent kiss;
The coy may struggle, but will grant the bliss:
The bliss obtain'd, the fictious struggle past,
Unbid, they'll clasp you in their arms at last.

THOUGH SHE'S THE GIRL

Though she's the girl, I am the one who's shy;
And though she walks with heavy hips, it's I
Who cannot move for heaviness; and she
Who is the woman: but the coward, me.
She is the one with high and swelling breast,
But I the one with weariness oppressed.
Clearly, in her the causal factors lie,
But the effects in me. I wonder why!

AMARU (5TH CENTURY),
TRANS. JOHN BROUGH

TO A YOUNG LADY, WITH
SOME LAMPREYS

With lovers 'twas of old the fashion
By presents to convey their passion;
No matter what the gift they sent,
The Lady saw that love was meant.
Fair *Atalanta*, as a favour,
Took the boar's head her Hero gave her;
Nor could the bristly thing affront her,
'Twas a fit present from a hunter.
When Squires send woodcocks to the dame,
It serves to show their absent flame:
Some by a snip of woven hair,
In posied lockets bribe the fair;
How many mercenary matches
Have sprung from Di'mond-rings and watches!
But hold – a ring, a watch, a locket,
Would drain at once a Poet's pocket;
He should send songs that cost him nought,
Nor ev'n he prodigal of thought.

Why then send Lampreys? fye, for shame!
'Twill set a virgin's blood on flame.
This to fifteen a proper gift!
It might lend sixty five a lift.

I know your maiden Aunt will scold,
And think my present somewhat bold.
I see her lift her hands and eyes.

  'What eat it, Niece? eat *Spanish* flies!
'Lamprey's a most immodest diet:
'You'll neither wake nor sleep in quiet.
'Should I to night eat Sago cream,
''Twould make me blush to tell my dream;
'If I eat Lobster, 'tis so warming,
'That ev'ry man I see looks charming;
'Wherefore had not the filthy fellow
'Laid *Rochester* upon your pillow?
'I vow and swear, I think the present
'Had been as modest and as decent.

  'Who has her virtue in her power?
'Each day has its unguarded hour;
'Always in danger of undoing,
'A prawn, a shrimp may prove our ruin!

  'The shepherdess, who lives on sallad,
'To cool her youth, controuls her palate;
'Should *Dian's* maids turn liqu'rish livers,
'And of huge lampreys rob the rivers,
'Then all beside each glade and Visto,
'You'd see Nymphs lying like *Calisto*.

'The man who meant to heat your blood,
'Needs not himself such vicious food –'
    In this, I own, your Aunt is clear,
I sent you what I well might spare:
For when I see you, (without joking)
Your eyes, lips, breasts, are so provoking,
They set my heart more cock-a-hoop,
Than could whole seas of craw-fish soupe.

THE SUCCUBUS

Thus will despair
In ecstasy of nightmare
Fetch you a devil-woman through the air,
  To slide below the sweated sheet
And kiss your lips in answer to your prayer
  And lock her hands with yours and your feet with
    her feet.

Yet why does she
Come never as longed-for beauty
Slender and cool, with limbs lovely to see,
  (The bedside candle guttering high)
And toss her head so the thick curls fall free
  Of halo'd breast, firm belly and long, slender thigh?

Why with hot face,
With paunched and uddered carcase,
Sudden and greedily does she embrace,
  Gulping away your soul, she lies so close,
Fathering brats on you of her own race?
  Yet is the fancy grosser than your lusts were gross?

ELEGY 9b

If I heard a voice from heaven say 'Live without
     loving,'
    I'd beg off. Girls are such exquisite hell.
When desire's slaked, when I'm sick of the whole
     business,
    Some kink in my wretched nature drives me back.
It's like riding a hard-mouthed horse, that bolts
     headlong, foam flying
    From his bit, and won't answer the rein –
Or being aboard a ship, on the point of docking, in
     harbour,
    When a sudden squall blows you back out to sea:
That's how the veering winds of desire so often catch
     me –
    Hot Love up to his lethal tricks again.
All right, boy, skewer me. I've dropped my defences,
    I'm an easy victim. Why, by now
Your arrows practically know their own way to the
     target
    And feel less at home in their quiver than in me.
I'm sorry for any fool who rates sleep a prime blessing
    And enjoys it from dusk to dawn
Night in, night out. What's sleep but cold death's
     reflection?
    Plenty of time for rest when you're in the grave.

My mistress deceives me – so what? I'd rather be lied to
    Than ignored. I can live on hope. Today
She'll be all endearments, tomorrow throw screaming
      tantrums,
    Envelop me one night, lock me out the next.
War, like love, is a toss-up. If Mars is inconstant, he
      gets that
    From you, his stepson. You're quite
Unpredictable, Cupid, with your lucky-dip favours,
    And more volatile than your own wings.
Maybe you'll hear my appeal, though – your delectable
      mother
    Might help there – and settle in as king of my heart?
Then admit the flighty sex *en masse* to your dominions
    And you'd have guaranteed popularity all round.

ODE 44

Last night, as half asleep I dreaming lay,
   Half naked came she in her little shift,
      With tilted glass, and verses on her lips;
Narcissus-eyes all shining for the fray,
      Filled full of frolic to her wine-red lips,
      Warm as a dewy rose, sudden she slips
   Into my bed – just in her little shift.

Said she, half naked, half asleep, half heard,
With a soft sigh betwixt each lazy word,
'Oh my old lover, do you sleep or wake!'
And instant I sat upright for her sake,
And drank whatever wine she poured for me –
Wine of the tavern, or vintage it might be
Of Heaven's own vine: he surely were a churl
Who refused wine poured out by such a girl,
A double traitor he to wine and love.
Go to, thou puritan! the gods above
Ordained this wine for us, but not for thee;
Drunkards we are by a divine decree,
Yea, by the special privilege of heaven
Foredoomed to drink and foreordained forgiven.

Ah! HAFIZ, you are not the only man
    Who promised penitence and broke down after;
For who can keep so hard a promise, man,
    With wine and woman brimming o'er with laughter!
O knotted locks, filled like a flower with scent,
How have you ravished this poor penitent!

THE EVE OF ST AGNES

St Agnes' Eve – Ah, bitter chill it was!
The owl, for all his feathers, was a-cold;
The hare limp'd trembling through the frozen grass,
And silent was the flock in woolly fold:
Numb were the Beadsman's fingers while he told
His rosary, and while his frosted breath,
Like pious incense from a censer old,
Seem'd taking flight for heaven, without a death,
Past the sweet Virgin's picture, while his prayer he
    saith.

His prayer he saith, this patient, holy man:
Then takes his lamp, and riseth from his knees,
And back returneth, meagre, barefoot, wan,
Along the chapel aisle by slow degrees:
The sculptured dead, on each side, seem to freeze,
Emprison'd in black, purgatorial rails:
Knights, ladies, praying in dumb orat'ries,
He passeth by, and his weak spirit fails
To think how they may ache in icy hoods and mails.

Northward he turneth through a little door,
  And scarce three steps, ere Music's golden tongue
Flatter'd to tears this aged man and poor.
  But no – already had his death-bell rung;
  The joys of all his life were said and sung;
  His was harsh penance on St Agnes' Eve:
  Another way he went, and soon among
  Rough ashes sat he for his soul's reprieve,
And all night kept awake, for sinners' sake to grieve.

That ancient Beadsman heard the prelude soft;
  And so it chanced, for many a door was wide,
  From hurry to and fro. Soon, up aloft,
  The silver, snarling trumpets 'gan to chide:
  The level chambers, ready with their pride,
  Were glowing to receive a thousand guests:
  The carvèd angels, ever eager-eyed,
  Stared, where upon their heads the cornice rests,
With hair blown back, and wings put crosswise on
    their breasts.

At length burst in the argent revelry,
With plume, tiara, and all rich array,
Numerous as shadows haunting fairly
The brain new-stuff'd, in youth, with triumphs gay
Of old romance. These let us wish away,
And turn, sole-thoughted, to one Lady there,
Whose heart had brooded, all that wintry day,
On love, and wing'd St Agnes' saintly care,
As she had heard old dames full many times declare.

They told her how, upon St Agnes' Eve,
Young virgins might have visions of delight,
And soft adorings from their loves receive
Upon the honey'd middle of the night,
If ceremonies due they did aright;
As, supperless to bed they must retire,
And couch supine their beauties, lily white;
Nor look behind, nor sideways, but require
Of Heaven with upward eyes for all that they desire.

Full of this whim was thoughtful Madeline:
The music, yearning like a God in pain,
She scarcely heard: her maiden eyes divine,
Fix'd on the floor, saw many a sweeping train
Pass by – she heeded not at all: in vain
Came many a tiptoe, amorous cavalier,
And back retired; not cool'd by high disdain,
But she saw not: her heart was otherwhere;
She sigh'd for Agnes' dreams, the sweetest of the year.

She danced along with vague, regardless eyes,
Anxious her lips, her breathing quick and short:
The hallow'd hour was near at hand: she sighs
Amid the timbrels, and the throng'd resort
Of whisperers in anger, or in sport;
'Mid looks of love, defiance, hate, and scorn,
Hoodwink'd with faery fancy; all amort,
Save to St Agnes and her lambs unshorn,
And all the bliss to be before to-morrow morn.

So, purposing each moment to retire,
  She linger'd still. Meantime, across the moors
Had come young Porphyro, with heart on fire
  For Madeline. Beside the portal doors,
Buttress'd from moonlight, stands he, and implores
  All saints to give him sight of Madeline,
But for one moment in the tedious hours,
  That he might gaze and worship all unseen;
Perchance speak, kneel, touch, kiss – in sooth such
      things have been.

He ventures in: let no buzz'd whisper tell,
  All eyes be muffled, or a hundred swords
Will storm his heart, Love's feverous citadel:
  For him, those chambers held barbarian hordes,
Hyena foemen, and hot-blooded lords,
  Whose very dogs would execrations howl
Against his lineage; not one breast affords
  Him any mercy in that mansion foul,
Save one old beldame, weak in body and in soul.

Ah, happy chance! the aged creature came,
Shuffling along with ivory-headed wand,
To where he stood, hid from the torch's flame,
Behind a broad hall pillar, far beyond
The sound of merriment and chorus bland.
He startled her: but soon she knew his face,
And grasp'd his fingers in her palsied hand,
Saying, 'Mercy, Porphyro! hie thee from his place;
They are all here to-night, the whole blood-thirsty
        race!

'Get hence! get hence! there's dwarfish Hildebrand:
He had a fever late, and in the fit
He cursèd thee and thine, both house and land:
Then there's that old Lord Maurice, not a whit
More tame for his grey hairs – Alas me! flit!
Flit like a ghost away.' – 'Ah, Gossip dear,
We're safe enough; here in this arm-chair sit,
And tell me how' – 'Good Saints! not here, not here;
Follow me, child, or else these stones will be thy bier.'

He follow'd through a lowly archèd way,
  Brushing the cobwebs with his lofty plume;
  And as she mutter'd 'Well-a – well-a-day!'
  He found him in a little moonlight room,
  Pale, latticed, chill, and silent as a tomb.
  'Now tell me where is Madeline,' said he,
  'O tell me, Angela, by the holy loom
  Which none but secret sisterhood may see,
When they St Agnes' wool are weaving piously.'

  'St Agnes! Ah! it is St Agnes' Eve –
  Yet men will murder upon holy days.
  Thou must hold water in a witch's sieve,
  And be liege-lord of all the Elves and Fays
  To venture so: it fills me with amaze
  To see thee, Porphyro! – St Agnes' Eve!
  God's help! my lady fair the conjurer plays
  This very night: good angels her deceive!
But let me laugh awhile, I've mickle time to grieve.'

Feebly she laugheth in the languid moon,
While Porphyro upon her face doth look,
Like puzzled urchin on an aged crone
Who keepeth closed a wondrous riddle-book,
As spectacled she sits in chimney nook.
But soon his eyes grew brilliant, when she told
His lady's purpose; and he scarce could brook
Tears, at the thought of those enchantments cold,
And Madeline asleep in lap of legends old.

Sudden a thought came like a full-blown rose,
Flushing his brow, and in his painèd heart
Made purple riot: then doth he propose
A stratagem, that makes the beldame start:
'A cruel man and impious thou art!
Sweet lady! let her pray, and sleep, and dream
Alone with her good angels, far apart
From wicked men like thee. Go, go! – I deem
Thou canst not surely be the same that thou didst
        seem.'

'I will not harm her, by all saints I swear!'
Quoth Porphyro: 'O may I ne'er find grace
When my weak voice shall whisper its last prayer,
If one of her soft ringlets I displace,
Or look with ruffian passion in her face.
Good Angela, believe me, by these tears;
Or I will, even in a moment's space,
Awake, with horrid shout, my foemen's ears,
And beard them, though they be more fang'd than
     wolves and bears.'

'Ah! why wilt thou affright a feeble soul?
A poor, weak, palsy-stricken, churchyard thing,
Whose passing-bell may ere the midnight toll;
Whose prayers for thee, each morn and evening,
Were never miss'd.' Thus plaining, doth she bring
A gentler speech from burning Porphyro;
So woeful, and of such deep sorrowing,
That Angela gives promise she will do
Whatever he shall wish, betide her weal or woe.

Which was, to lead him, in close secrecy,
Even to Madeline's chamber, and there hide
Him in a closet, of such privacy
That he might see her beauty unespied,
And win perhaps that night a peerless bride,
While legion'd fairies paced the coverlet,
And pale enchantment held her sleepy-eyed.
Never on such a night have lovers met,
Since Merlin paid his Demon all the monstrous debt.

'It shall be as thou wishest,' said the Dame:
'All cates and dainties shall be storèd there
Quickly on this feast-night: by the tambour frame
Her own lute thou wilt see: no time to spare,
For I am slow and feeble, and scarce dare
On such a catering trust my dizzy head.
Wait here, my child, with patience; kneel in prayer
The while. Ah! thou must needs the lady wed,
Or may I never leave my grave among the dead.'

So saying, she hobbled off with busy fear.
The lover's endless minutes slowly pass'd;
The dame return'd, and whisper'd in his ear
To follow her; with aged eyes aghast
From fright of dim espial. Safe at last
Through many a dusky gallery, they gain
The maiden's chamber, silken, hush'd, and chaste;
Where Porphyro took covert, pleased amain.
His poor guide hurried back with agues in her brain.

Her faltering hand upon the balustrade,
Old Angela was feeling for the stair,
When Madeline, St Agnes' charmèd maid,
Rose, like a mission'd spirit, unaware:
With silver taper's light, and pious care,
She turn'd, and down the aged gossip led
To a safe level matting. Now prepare,
Young Porphyro, for gazing on that bed;
She comes, she comes again, like ring-dove fray'd and
    fled.

Out went the taper as she hurried in;
Its little smoke, in pallid moonshine, died:
She closed the door, she panted, all akin
To spirits of the air, and visions wide:
No utter'd syllable, or, woe betide!
But to her heart, her heart was voluble,
Paining with eloquence her balmy side;
As though a tongueless nightingale should swell
Her throat in vain, and die, heart-stifled, in her dell.

A casement high and triple-arch'd there was,
All garlanded with carven imageries,
Of fruits and flowers, and bunches of knot-grass,
And diamonded with panes of quaint device,
Innumerable of stains and spendid dyes,
As are the tiger-moth's deep-damask'd wings;
And in the midst, 'mong thousand heraldries,
And twilight saints, and dim emblazonings,
A shielded scutcheon blush'd with blood of queens and
    kings.

Full on this casement shone the wintry moon,
And threw warm gules on Madeline's fair breast,
As down she knelt for Heaven's grace and boon;
Rose-bloom fell on her hands, together prest,
And on her silver cross soft amethyst,
And on her hair a glory, like a saint:
She seem'd a splendid angel, newly drest,
Save wings, for heaven: – Porphyro grew faint:
She knelt, so pure a thing, so free from mortal taint.

Anon his heart revives: her vespers done,
Of all its wreathèd pearls her hair she frees;
Unclasps her warmèd jewels one by one;
Loosens her fragrant boddice; by degrees
Her rich attire creeps rustling to her knees:
Half-hidden, like a mermaid in sea-weed,
Pensive awhile she dreams awake, and sees,
In fancy, fair St Agnes in her bed,
But dares not look behind, or all the charm is fled.

Soon, trembling in her soft and chilly nest,
    In sort of wakeful swoon, perplex'd she lay,
Until the poppied warmth of sleep oppress'd
    Her soothed limbs, and soul fatigued away.
Flown, like a thought, until the morrow-day;
    Blissfully haven'd both from joy and pain;
Clasp'd like a missal where swart Paynims pray;
    Blinded alike from sunshine and from rain,
As though a rose should shut, and be a bud again.

Stolen to this paradise, and so entranced,
    Porphyro gazed upon her empty dress,
And listen'd to her breathing, if it chanced
    To wake into a slumberous tenderness;
Which when he heard, that minute did he bless,
    And breath'd himself: then from the closet crept,
Noiseless as fear in a wide wilderness,
    And over the hush'd carpet, silent, stept,
And 'tween the curtains peep'd, where, lo! – how fast
    she slept!

Then by the bed-side, where the faded moon
Made a dim, silver twilight, soft he set
A table, and, half anguish'd, threw thereon
A cloth of woven crimson, gold, and jet: —
O for some drowsy Morphean amulet!
The boisterous, midnight, festive clarion,
The kettle-drum, and far-heard clarionet,
Affray his ears, though but in dying tone: —
The hall-door shuts again, and all the noise is gone.

And still she slept an azure-lidded sleep,
In blanchèd linen, smooth, and lavender'd,
While he from forth the closet brought a heap
Of candied apple, quince, and plum, and gourd;
With jellies soother than the creamy curd,
And lucent syrops, tinct with cinnamon;
Manna and dates, in argosy transferr'd
From Fez; and spicèd dainties, every one,
From silken Samarcand to cedar'd Lebanon.

These delicates he heap'd with glowing hand
On golden dishes and in baskets bright
Of wreathèd silver: sumptuous they stand
In the retired quiet of the night,
Filling the chilly room with perfume light. –
'And now, my love, my seraph fair, awake!
Thou art my heaven, and I thine eremite:
Open thine eyes, for meek St Agnes' sake,
Or I shall drowse beside thee, so my soul doth ache.'

Thus whispering, his warm, unnervèd arm
Sank in her pillow. Shaded was her dream
By the dusk curtains: – 'twas a midnight charm
Impossible to melt as icèd stream:
The lustrous salvers in the moonlight gleam;
Broad golden fringe upon the carpet lies:
It seem'd he never, never could redeem
From such a steadfast spell his lady's eyes;
So mused awhile, entoil'd in woofèd phantasies.

Awakening up, he took her hollow lute, —
Tumultuous, — and, in chords that tenderest be,
He play'd an ancient ditty, long since mute,
In Provence call'd 'La belle dame sans mercy':
Close to her ear touching the melody; —
Wherewith disturb'd, she utter'd a soft moan:
He ceased — she panted quick   and suddenly
Her blue affrayèd eyes wide open shone:
Upon his knees he sank, pale as smooth-sculptured
     stone.

Her eyes were open, but she still beheld,
Now wide awake, the vision of her sleep:
There was a painful change, that nigh expell'd
The blisses of her dream so pure and deep.
At which fair Madeline began to weep,
And moan forth witless words with many a sigh,
While still her gaze on Porphyro would keep;
Who knelt, with joinèd hands and piteous eye,
Fearing to move or speak, she look'd so dreamingly.

'Ah, Porphyro!' said she, 'but even now
Thy voice was at sweet tremble in mine ear,
Made tunable with every sweetest vow;
And those sad eyes were spiritual and clear:
How changed thou art! how pallid, chill, and drear!
Give me that voice again, my Porphyro,
Those looks immortal, those complainings dear!
O leave me not in this eternal woe,
For if thou diest, my Love, I know not where to go.'

Beyond a mortal man impassion'd far
At these voluptuous accents, he arose,
Ethereal, flush'd, and like a throbbing star
Seen 'mid the sapphire heaven's deep repose;
Into her dream he melted, as the rose
Blendeth its odour with the violet, –
Solution sweet: meantime the frost-wind blows
Like Love's alarum pattering the sharp sleet
Against the window-panes; St Agnes' moon hath set.

'Tis dark: quick pattereth the flaw-blown sleet,
'This is no dream, my bride, my Madeline!'
'Tis dark: the icèd gusts still rave and beat:
'No dream, alas! alas! and woe is mine!
Porphyro will leave me here to fade and pine.
Cruel! what traitor could thee hither bring?
I curse not, for my heart is lost in thine,
Though thou forsakest a deceivèd thing; –
A dove forlorn and lost with sick unprunèd wing.'

'My Madeline! sweet dreamer! lovely bride!
Say, may I be for aye thy vassal blest?
Thy beauty's shield, heart-shaped and
     vermeil-dyed?
Ah, silver shrine, here will I take my rest
After so many hours of toil and quest,
A famish'd pilgrim, – saved by miracle.
Though I have found, I will not rob thy nest,
Saving of thy sweet self; if thou think'st well
To trust, fair Madeline, to no rude infidel.

'Hark! 'tis an elfin storm from faery land,
Of haggard seeming, but a boon indeed:
Arise – arise! the morning is at hand; –
The bloated wassailers will never heed: –
Let us away, my love, with happy speed;
There are no ears to hear, or eyes to see, –
Drown'd all in Rhenish and the sleepy mead.
Awake! arise! my love, and fearless be,
For o'er the southern moors I have a home for thee.'

She hurried at his words, beset with fears,
For there were sleeping dragons all around,
At glaring watch, perhaps, with ready spears.
Down the wide stairs a darkling way they found;
In all the house was heard no human sound.
A chain-droop'd lamp was flickering by each door;
The arras, rich with horsemen, hawk, and hound,
Flutter'd in the besieging wind's uproar;
And the long carpets rose along the gusty floor.

They glide, like phantoms, into the wide hall;
Like phantoms to the iron porch they glide,
Where lay the Porter, in uneasy sprawl,
With a huge empty flagon by his side:
The wakeful bloodhound rose, and shook his hide,
But his sagacious eye an inmate owns:
By one, and one, the bolts full easy slide: –
The chains lie silent on the footworn stones;
The key turns, and the door upon its hinges groans.

And they are gone: ay, ages long ago
These lovers fled away into the storm.
That night the Baron dreamt of many a woe,
And all his warrior-guests with shade and form
Of witch, and demon, and large coffin-worm,
Were long be-nightmared. Angela the old
Died palsy-twitch'd, with meagre face deform;
The Beadsman, after thousand aves told,
For aye unsought-for slept among his ashes cold.

FIGS

The proper way to eat a fig, in society,
Is to split it in four, holding it by the stump,
And open it, so that it is a glittering, rosy, moist,
    honied, heavy-petalled four-petalled flower.

Then you throw away the skin
Which is just like a four-petalled calex,
After you have taken off the blossom with your lips.

But the vulgar way
Is just to put your mouth to the crack, and take out the
    flesh in one bite.

Every fruit has its secret.
The fig is a very secretive fruit.
As you see it standing growing, you feel at once it is
    symbolic:
And it seems male.
But when you come to know it better, you agree with
    the Romans, it is female.

The Italians vulgarly say, it stands for the female part;
    the fig-fruit:
The fissure, the yoni,
The wonderful moist conductivity towards the centre.

Involved,
Inturned,
The flowering all inward and womb-fibrilled;
And but one orifice.

The fig, the horse-shoe, the squash-blossom.
Symbols.

There was a flower that flowered inward, womb-ward;
Now there is a fruit like a ripe womb.
It was always a secret.
That's how it should be, the female should always be
     secret.

There never was any standing aloft and unfolded on a
     bough
Like other flowers, in a revelation of petals;
Silver-pink peach, venetian glass of medlars and
     sorb-apples,
Shallow wine-cups on short, bulging stems
Openly pledging heaven:
Here's to the thorn in flower! Here is to Utterance!
The brave, adventurous rosaceae.

Folded upon itself, and secret unutterable,
And milk-sapped, sap that curdles milk and makes
    ricotta,
Sap that smells strange on your fingers, that even
    goats won't taste it;
Folded upon itself, enclosed like any Mohammedan
    woman,
Its nakedness all within-walls, its flowering forever
    unseen,
One small way of access only, and this close-curtained
    from the light;
Fig, fruit of the female mystery, covert and inward,
Mediterranean fruit, with your covert nakedness,
Where everything happens invisible, flowering and
    fertilisation, and fruiting
In the inwardness of your you, that eye will never see
Till it's finished, and you're over-ripe, and you burst to
    give up your ghost.

Till the drop of ripeness exudes,
And the year is over.

That's how the fig dies, showing her crimson through
    the purple slit
Like a wound, the exposure of her secret, on the open day.
Like a prostitute, the bursten fig, making a show of her
    secret.

That's how women die too.

The year is fallen over-ripe,
The year of our women.
The year of our women is fallen over-ripe.
The secret is laid bare.
And rottenness soon sets in.
The year of our women is fallen over-ripe.

When Eve once knew *in her mind* that she was naked
She quickly sewed fig-leaves, and sewed the same for
     the man.
She'd been naked all her days before,
But still then, till that apple of knowledge, she hadn't
     had the fact on her mind.

She got the fact on her mind, and quickly sewed
     fig-leaves.
And women have been sewing ever since.
But now they stitch to adorn the bursten fig, not to
     cover it.
They have their nakedness more than ever on their
     mind,
And they won't let us forget it.
Now, the secret
Becomes an affirmation through moist, scarlet lips
That laugh at the Lord's indignation.

What then, good Lord! cry the women.
We have kept our secret long enough.
We are a ripe fig.
Let us burst into affirmation.

They forget, ripe figs won't keep.
Ripe figs won't keep.

Honey-white figs of the north, black figs with scarlet
      inside, of the south.
Ripe figs won't keep, won't keep in any clime.
What then, when women the world over have all
      bursten into self-assertion?
And bursten figs won't keep?

NATIONAL WINTER GARDEN

Outspoken buttocks in pink beads
Invite the necessary cloudy clinch
Of bandy eyes. . . . No extra mufflings here:
The world's one flagrant, sweating cinch.

And while legs waken salads in the brain
You pick your blonde out neatly through the smoke.
Always you wait for someone else though, always –
(Then rush the nearest exit through the smoke).

Always and last, before the final ring
When all the fireworks blare, begins
A tom-tom scrimmage with a somewhere violin,
Some cheapest echo of them all – begins.

And shall we call her whiter than the snow?
Sprayed first with ruby, then with emerald sheen –
Least tearful and least glad (who knows her smile?)
A caught slide shows her sandstone grey between.

Her eyes exist in swivellings of her teats,
Pearls whip her hips, a drench of whirling strands.
Her silly snake rings begin to mount, surmount
Each other – turquoise fakes on tinselled hands.

We wait that writhing pool, her pearls collapsed,
– All but her belly buried in the floor;
And the lewd trounce of a final muted beat!
We feel her spasm through a fleshless door. . . .

Yet, to the empty trapeze of your flesh,
O Magdalene, each comes back to die alone.
Then you, the burlesque of our lust – and faith,
Lug us back lifeward – bone by infant bone.

A NOTE ON PROPERTIUS 1.5

Among the Roman love-poets, possession
Is a rare theme. The locked and flower-hung door,
The shivering lover, are allowed. To more
Buoyant moods, the canons of expression
Gave grudging sanction. Do we, then, assume,
Finding Propertius tear-sodden and jealous,
That Cynthia was inexorably callous?
Plenty of moonlight entered that high room
Whose doors had met his Alexandrine battles;
And she, so gay a lutanist, was known
To stitch and doze a night away, alone,
Until the poet tumbled in with apples
For penitence and for her head his wreath,
Brought from a party, of wine-scented roses –
(The garland's aptness lying, one supposes,
Less in the flowers than in the thorns beneath:
Her waking could, he knew, provide his verses
With less idyllic themes.) Onto her bed
He rolled the round fruit, and adorned her head;
Then gently roused her sleeping mouth to curses.
Here the conventions reassert their power:

The apples fall and bruise, the roses wither,
Touched by a sallowed moon. But there were other
Luminous nights – (even the cactus flower
Glows briefly golden, fed by spiny flesh) –
And once, as he acknowledged all was singing:
The moonlight musical, the darkness clinging,
And she compliant to his every wish.

SEXUAL COUPLETS

Here we are, without our clothes,
one excited watering can, one peculiar rose ...

My shoe-tree wants to come,
and stretch your body where it lies undone ...

I am wearing a shiny sou'wester;
you are coxcombed like a jester ...

Oh my strangely gutted one,
the fish head needs your flesh around its bone ...

We move in anapaestic time and pause,
until my body rhymes with yours ...

In the valley of your arse,
all flesh is grass, all flesh is grass ...

One damp acorn on the tweedy sod –
then the broad bean dangles in its pod ...

CRAIG RAINE (1944–   )   137

FOR MY WIFE

A charming girl, full of dejected love,
Weaves plain silk as autumn sounds stir.
Passing the yarn-guide her bracelet jade trembles,
Pressing the shears her belt pearls tinkle.
Warp so fine threatens to jam the shuttle,
Woof snaps, she's cross the silk is too thin.
Grapevine begins to look finished,
Mandarin ducks have yet to emerge.

Under cloudy ridge-poles all the weavers stroll,
Silk windows open to each other.
Through window grilles float eyebrow whispers,
From silk to light come smiling eyes.
Blurred, screened by thinnest silk,
Yet clearly glimpsed cosmetic flower:
Sweetheart lotus roots studded with jade,
Loveknot flowers strung with jewels,
Her red gown fastened at the back,
Gold pins slant toward her sidecurls.
From the loom top hangs gay braid,
From the loom's side cascade strings of pearls.
Green silk threads draw in the pivot's crouching hare,
Yellow gold encirles the pulley's Lulu knob.
Rich tints dart from her skirt hem,
Scented gloss glistens on her lips.

One-hundred-city barons ask after her,
Five-horse teams paw the ground before her.

There is only me in my bedroom,
Faithful to past love, not seeking new amours.
In dreams weeping soaks my flowery pillow,
Waking tears drench my silk kerchief.
Sleeping alone is so hard for me,
My double quilt still feels cold.
Even more I desire your skin's marbrous warmth,
More than ever long for horizontal pleasures.

LIU HSIAO-WEI (5TH CENTURY),   139
TRANS. ANNE BIRRELL

LOVE AND THE CREATURES

Thus every Creature, and of every Kind,
The secret Joys of sweet Coition find:
Not only Man's Imperial Race; but they
That wing the liquid Air, or swim the Sea,
Or haunt the Desart, rush into the flame:
For Love is Lord of all; and is in all the same.
'Tis with this rage, the Mother Lion stung,
Scours o're the Plain; regardless of her young:
Demanding Rites of Love, she sternly stalks;
And hunts her Lover in his lonely Walks.
'Tis then the shapeless Bear his Den forsakes;
In Woods and Fields a wild destruction makes.
Boars whet their Tusks; to battle Tygers move;
Enrag'd with hunger, more enrag'd with love.
Then wo to him, that in the desert Land
Of Lybia travels, o're the burning Sand.
The Stallion snuffs the well-known Scent afar;
And snorts and trembles for the distant Mare:
Nor Bitts nor Bridles, can his rage restrain;
And rugged Rocks are interpos'd in vain:

He makes his way o're Mountains, and contemns
Unruly Torrents, and unfooded Streams.
The bristled Boar, who feels the pleasing wound,
New grinds his arming Tusks, and digs the ground.
The sleepy Leacher shuts his little Eyes;
About his churning Chaps the frothy bubbles rise:
He rubs his sides against a Tree; prepares
And hardens both his Shoulders for the Wars.

MADRIGAL

Like the Idalian queen,
Her hair about her eyne,
With neck and breast's ripe apples to be seen,
At first glance of the morn
In Cyprus' gardens gathering those fair flowers
Which of her blood were born,
I saw, but fainting saw, my paramours.
The Graces naked danced about the place,
The winds and trees amazed
With silence on her gazed,
The flowers did smile, like those upon her face;
And as their aspen stalks those fingers band,
That she might read my case,
A hyacinth I wished me in her hand.

ROMAN ELEGY Ia

Fortune beyond my loveliest daydreams fulfilled is my
    own now,
    Amor, my clever guide, passed all the palaces by.
Long he has known, and I too had occasion to learn by
    experience,
    What a richly gilt room hides behind hangings and
    screens.
You may call him a boy and blind and ill-mannered,
    but, clever
    Amor, I know you well, never corruptible god!
Us they did not take in, those façades so imposing and
    pompous,
    Gallant balcony here, dignified courtyard down
    there.
Quickly we passed them by, and a humble but delicate
    doorway
    Opened to guided and guide, made them both
    welcome within.
All he provides for me there, with his help I obtain all I
    ask for,
    Fresher roses each day strewn on my path by the god.
Isn't it heaven itself? – And what more could the lovely
    Borghese,
    Nipotima herself offer a lover than that?
Dinners, drives and dances, operas, card games and
    parties,

Often merely they steal Amor's most opportune
hours.
Airs and finery bore me; when all's said and done, it's
the same thing
Whether the skirt you lift is of brocade or of wool.
Or if the wish of a girl is to pillow her lover in comfort,
Wouldn't he first have her put all those sharp
trinkets away?
All those jewels and pads, and the lace that surrounds
her, the whalebone,
Don't they all have to go, if he's to feel his beloved?
Us it gives much less trouble! Your plain woollen dress
in a jiffy,
Unfastened by me, slips down, lies in its folds on the
floor.
Quickly I carry the child in her flimsy wrapping of
linen,
As befits a good nurse, teasingly, into her bed.
Bare of silken drapery, mattresses richly embroidered,
Spacious enough for two, free in a wide room it
stands.
Then let Jupiter get more joy from his Juno, a mortal
Anywhere in this world know more contentment
than I.
We enjoy the delights of the genuine naked god, Amor,
And our rock-a-bye bed's rhythmic, melodious
creak.

144   J. W. VON GOETHE (1749–1832),
      TRANS. MICHAEL HAMBURGER

ANOINTED VESSEL

Admire the watered silky gap,
Mahomet's paradise, that shows
My creamy entry through the lap
Of luxuries that once were rose.

Oh, tired old eyes, take up delight
As painters do, forget your tears
Though warranted, in this rich sight –
This vessel that uplifts and cheers:

In a soft box of plushy fluff,
Black, but with glints of copper-red
And edges crinkly like a ruff,
Lies the great god of gems in bed,

Throbbing with sap and life, and sends
In wafts the best news ever sent,
A perfume his ecstatic friends
Think stolen from each element.

But contemplate this temple cont-
emplate, then get your breath, and kiss
The jewel having fits in front,
The ruby grinning for its bliss,

Flower of the inner court, kid brother
So mad about the taller one
It kisses till they both half-smother
And puff, then pulse, in unison . . .

But rest; you're blazing now; relax.
It too should calm and cool; but rest? –
In those embrasures and hot cracks
Of thigh and belly, breast and breast?

No, soon its straying tipsiness
Wins my parts over to a man.
My flesh stands up and nods: right dress!
Begin again where we began.

HIMALAYAN BALSAM

Orchid-lipped, loose-jointed, purplish, indolent
    flowers,
with a ripe smell of peaches, like a girl's breath
    through lipstick,
delicate and coarse in the weedlap of late summer
    rivers,
dishevelled, weak-stemmed, common as brambles, as
    love which

subtracts us from seasons, their courtships and
    murders,
(*Meta segmentata* in her web, and the male waiting,
between blossom and violent blossom, meticulous
    spiders
repeated in gossamer, and the slim males waiting ...)

Fragrance too rich for keeping, too light to remember,
like grief for the cat's sparrow and the wild gull's
beach-hatched embryo. (She ran from the reaching
    water
with the broken egg in her hand, but the clamped bill

refused brandy and grubs, a shred too naked and
        perilous for
life offered freely in cardboard boxes, little windowsill
coffins for bird death, kitten death, squirrel death,
        summer
repeated and ended in heartbreak, in the sad small
        funerals.)

Sometimes, shaping bread or scraping potatoes for
        supper,
I have stood in the kitchen, transfixed by what I'd call
        love
if love were a whiff, a wanting for no particular lover,
no child, or baby or creature. 'Love, dear love'

I could cry to these scent-spilling ragged flowers
and mean nothing but 'no', by that word's breadth,
to their evident going, their important descent
        through red towering
stalks to the riverbed. It's not, as I thought, that death

creates love. More that love knows death. Therefore
tears, therefore poems, therefore the long stone sobs of
     cathedrals
that speak to no ferret or fox, that prevent no
     massacre.
(I am combing abundant leaves from these icy
     shallows.)

Love, it was you who said, 'Murder the killer
we have to call life and we'd be a bare planet under a
     dead sun.'
Then I loved you with the usual soft lust of October
that says 'yes' to the coming winter and a summoning
     odour of balsam.

DOWN, WANTON, DOWN!

Down, wanton, down! Have you no shame
That at the whisper of Love's name,
Or Beauty's, presto! up you raise
Your angry head and stand at gaze?

Poor Bombard-captain, sworn to reach
The ravelin and effect a breach –
Indifferent what you storm or why,
So be that in the breach you die!

Love may be blind, but Love at least
Knows what is man and what mere beast;
Or Beauty wayward, but requires
More delicacy from her squires.

Tell me, my witless, whose one boast
Could be your staunchness at the post,
When were you made a man of parts
To think fine and profess the arts?

Will many-gifted Beauty come
Bowing to your bald rule of thumb,
Or Love swear loyalty to your crown?
Be gone, have done! Down, wanton, down!

MODES OF PLEASURE

New face, strange face, for my unrest.
I hunt your look, and lust marks time
Dark in his doubtful uniform,
Preparing once more for the test.

You do not know you are observed:
Apart, contained, you wait on chance,
Or seem to, till your callous glance
Meets mine, as callous and reserved.

And as it does we recognize
That sharing an anticipation
Amounts to a collaboration –
A warm game for a warmer prize.

Yet when I've had you once or twice
I may not want you any more:
A single night is plenty for
Every magnanimous device.

Why should that matter? Why pretend
Love must accompany erection?
This is a momentary affection,
A curiosity bound to end,

Which as good-humoured muscle may
Against the muscle try its strength
– Exhausted into sleep at length –
And will not last long into day.

THE POSTURE

Of like importance is the posture too,
In which the genial feat of Love we do:
For as the Females of the four foot kind,
Receive the leapings of their Males behind;
So the good Wives, with loins uplifted high,
And leaning on their hands and fruitful stroke may try:
For in that posture will they best conceive:
Not when supinely laid they frisk and heave;
For active motions only break the blow,
And more of Strumpets than of Wives they show;
When answering stroke with stroke, the mingled
    liquors flow.
Endearments eager, and too brisk a bound,
Throws off the Plow-share from the furrow'd ground.
But common Harlots in conjunction heave,
Because 'tis less their business to conceive
Than to delight, and to provoke the deed;
A trick which honest Wives but little need.

Nor is it from the Gods, or Cupids dart,
That many a homely Woman takes the heart;
But Wives well humour'd, dutiful, and chaste,
And clean, will hold their wandring Husbands fast,
Such are the links of Love, and such a Love will last.
For what remains, long habitude, and use,
Will kindness in domestick Bands produce:
For Custome will a strong impression leave;
Hard bodies, which the lightest stroke receive,
In length of time, will moulder and decay,
And stones with drops of rain are wash'd away.

LUCRETIUS (*c.* 99–55 BC),
TRANS. JOHN DRYDEN

THE NAKED AND THE NUDE

For me, the naked and the nude
(By lexicographers construed
As synonyms that should express
The same deficiency of dress
Or shelter) stand as wide apart
As love from lies, or truth from art.

Lovers without reproach will gaze
On bodies naked and ablaze;
The Hippocratic eye will see
In nakedness, anatomy;
And naked shines the Goddess when
She mounts her lion among men.

The nude are bold, the nude are sly
To hold each treasonable eye.
While draping by a showman's trick
Their dishabille in rhetoric,
They grin a mock-religious grin
Of scorn at those of naked skin.

The naked, therefore, who compete
Against the nude may know defeat;
Yet when they both together tread
The briary pastures of the dead,
By Gorgons with long whips pursued,
How naked go the sometime nude!

IN NATURE THERE IS NEITHER
RIGHT NOR LEFT NOR WRONG

Men are what they do, women are what they are.
These erect breasts, like marble coming up for air
Among the cataracts of my breathtaking hair,
Are goods in my bazaar, a door ajar
To the first paradise of whores and mothers.

Men buy their way back into me from the upright
Right-handed puzzle that men fit together
From their deeds, the pieces. Women shoot from
Or dive back into its interstices
As squirrels inhabit a geometry.

We women sell ourselves for sleep, for flesh,
To those wide-awake, successful spirits, men —
Who, lying each midnight with the sinister
Beings, their dark companions, women,
Suck childhood, beasthood, from a mother's breasts.

A fat bald rich man comes home at twilight
And lectures me about my parking tickets; gowned in
     gold
Lamé, I look at him and think: 'You're old,
I'm old.' Husband, I sleep with you every night
And like it; but each morning when I wake
I've dreamed of my first love, the subtle serpent.

SHE BRINGS THE SURPRISE
OF BEING

She brings the surprise of being.
Is tall, a subdued gold.
Simply to think of seeing
Her half-mature body does good.

Her tall breasts would seem two
Hills (were she lying down)
Dawning without going through
Any twilight dawn.

The hand of her white arm settles,
Its span spread wide, to press
Lightly her side – the subtle
Swelling of her form in the dress.

She's tempting like a boat.
Has something of bud and shoot.
God! when do I go aboard?
Hunger! when is it I eat?

FERNANDO PESSOA (1888–1935),
TRANS. JONATHAN GRIFFIN

THE MILKMAID'S EPITHALAMIUM

Joy to the bridegroom and the bride
That lie by one another's side!
O fie upon the virgin beds,
No loss is gain but maidenheads.
Love quickly send the time may be
When I shall deal my rosemary!

I long to simper at a feast,
To dance, and kiss, and do the rest.
When I shall wed, and bedded be
O then the qualm comes over me,
And tells the sweetness of a theme
That I ne'er knew but in a dream.

You ladies have the blessed nights,
I pine in hope of such delights.
And silly damsel only can
Milk the cows' teats and think on man:
And sigh and wish to taste and prove
The wholesome sillabub of love.

Make haste, at once twin-brothers bear;
And leave new matter for a star.
Women and ships are never shown
So fair as when their sails be blown.
Then when the midwife hears your moan,
I'll sigh for grief that I have none.

And you, dear knight, whose every kiss
Reaps the full crop of Cupid's bliss,
Now you have found, confess and tell
That single sheets do make up hell.
And then so charitable be
To get a man to pity me.

SITTING OUT NEW YEAR WITH MY WIFE

Pleasure sweet, excitement without end,
Joy sublime – don't stop the winecups!
From wine we fish daddy-longlegs,
In rice dumplings we search for wild plum.
Blinds open, winds come through the curtains,
Candles die, charcoal burns to ash.
'No wonder pins feel heavy in your curls –
It's from waiting till dawn light comes.'

SECULAR ELEGY V

O Golden Fleece she is where she lies tonight
Trammelled in her sheets like midsummer on a bed,
Kisses like moths flitter over her bright
Mouth, and, as she turns her head,
All space moves over to give her beauty room.

Where her hand, like a bird on the branch of her arm,
Droops its wings over the bedside as she sleeps,
There the air perpetually stays warm
Since, nested, her hand rested there. And she keeps
Under her green thumb life like a growing poem.

My nine-tiered tigress in the cage of sex
I feed with meat that you tear from my side
Crowning your nine months with the paradox:
The love that kisses with a homicide
In robes of red generation resurrects.

The bride who rides the hymenæal waterfall
Spawning all possibles in her pools of surplus,
Whom the train rapes going into a tunnel,
The imperial multiplicator nothing can nonplus:
My mother Nature is the origin of it all.

At Pharaoh's Feast and in the family cupboard,
Gay corpse, bright skeleton, and the fly in amber,
She sits with her laws like antlers from her forehead
Enmeshing everyone, with flowers and thunder
Adorning the head that destiny never worried.

ULYSSES

To the much-tossed Ulysses, never done
    With woman whether gowned as wife or whore,
Penelope and Circe seemed as one:
She like a whore made his lewd fancies run,
    And wifely she a hero to him bore.

Their counter-changings terrified his way:
    They were the clashing rocks, Symplegades,
Scylla and Charybdis too were they;
Now angry storms frosting the sea with spray
    And now the lotus island's drunken ease.

They multiplied into the Sirens' throng,
    Forewarned by fear of whom he stood bound fast
Hand and foot helpless to the vessel's mast,
Yet would not stop his ears: daring their song
    He groaned and sweated till that shore was past.

One, two and many: flesh had made him blind,
    Flesh had one pleasure only in the act,
Flesh set one purpose only in the mind –
Triumph of flesh and afterwards to find
    Still those same terrors wherewith flesh was racked.

His wiles were witty and his fame far known,
Every king's daughter sought him for her own,
    Yet he was nothing to be won or lost.
    All lands to him were Ithaca: love-tossed
He loathed the fraud, yet would not bed alone.

WE DID IT

We did it in front of the mirror
And in the light. We did it in darkness,
In water, and in the high grass.

We did it in honour of man
And in honour of beast and in honour of God.
But they didn't want to know about us,
They'd already seen our sort.

We did it with imagination and colours,
With confusion of reddish hair and brown
And with difficult gladdening
Exercises. We did it

Like wheels and holy creatures
And with chariot-feats of prophets.
We did it six wings
And six legs.
        But the heavens
Were hard above us
Like the earth of the summer beneath.

YEHUDA AMICHAI (1924–   ),   167
TRANS. HAROLD SCHIMMEL

NO, NEVER THINK

No, never think, my dear, that in my heart I treasure
The tumult of the blood, the frenzied gusts of pleasure,
Those groans of hers, those shrieks: a young
    Bacchante's cries,
When writing like a snake in my embrace she lies,
And wounding kiss and touch, urgent and hot,
    engender
The final shudderings that consummate surrender.
How sweeter far are you, my meek, my quiet one,
By what tormenting bliss is my whole soul undone
When, after I have long and eagerly been pleading,
With bashful graciousness to my deep need conceding,
You give yourself to me, but shyly, turned away,
To all my ardors cold, scarce heeding what I say,
Responding, growing warm, oh, in how slow a fashion,
To share, unwilling, yet to share at last my passion!

THE FLEA

   Mark but this flea, and mark in this,
How little that which thou deny'st me is;
   Me it sucked first, and now sucks thee,
And in this flea, our two bloods mingled be;
   Confess it, this cannot be said
A sin, or shame, or loss of maidenhead,
   Yet this enjoys before it woo,
And pampered swells with one blood made of two,
And this, alas, is more than we would do.

   Oh stay, three lives in one flea spare,
Where we almost, nay more than married are:
   This flea is you and I, and this
Our marriage bed, and marriage temple is;
   Though parents grudge, and you, we're met,
And cloistered in these living walls of jet.
   Though use make thee apt to kill me,
Let not to this, self murder added be,
And sacrilege, three sins in killing three.

Cruel and sudden, hast thou since
Purpled thy nail, in blood of innocence?
  In what could this flea guilty be,
Except in that drop which it sucked from thee?
  Yet thou triumph'st, and say'st that thou
Find'st not thyself, nor me the weaker now;
    'Tis true, then learn how false, fears be;
Just so much honour, when thou yield'st to me,
Will waste, as this flea's death took life from thee.

TO ANTHEA

Let's call for Hymen if agreed thou art —
Delays in love but crucify the heart.
Love's thorny tapers yet neglected lie;
Speak thou the word, they'll kindle by and by.
The nimble hours woo us on to wed,
And Genius waits to have us both to bed.
Behold, for us the naked Graces stay
With maunds of roses for to strew the way.
Besides, the most religious prophet stands
Ready to join as well our hearts as hands.
June yet smiles; but if she chance to chide,
Ill luck 'twill bode to th'bridegroom and the bride.
Tell me Anthea, dost thou fondly dread
The loss of that we call a maidenhead?
Come, I'll instruct thee. Know, the vestal fire
Is not by marriage quenched, but flames the higher.

ROBERT HERRICK (1591—1674)

COUNTERPARTS

In my body you search the mountain
for the sun buried in its forest.
In your body I search for the boat
adrift in the middle of the night.

ON THE MARRIAGE OF A VIRGIN

Waking alone in a multitude of loves when morning's
    light
Surprised in the opening of her nightlong eyes
His golden yesterday asleep upon the iris
And this day's sun leapt up the sky out of her thighs
Was miraculous virginity old as loaves and fishes,
Though the moment of a miracle is unending
    lightning
And the shipyards of Galilee's footprints hide a navy of
    doves.

No longer will the vibrations of the sun desire on
Her deepsea pillow where once she married alone,
Her heart all ears and eyes, lips catching the avalanche
Of the golden ghost who ringed with his streams her
    mercury bone,
Who under the lids of her windows hoisted his golden
    luggage,
For a man sleeps where fire leapt down and she learns
    through his arm
That other sun, the jealous coursing of the unrivalled
    blood.

DYLAN THOMAS (1914–1953)   173

THE METAPHOR

The act of love seemed a dead metaphor
For love itself, until the timeless moment
When fingers trembled, heads clouded,
And love rode everywhere, too numinous
To be expressed or greeted calmly:
O, then it was, deep in our own forest,
We dared revivify the metaphor,
Shedding the garments of this epoch
In scorn of time's wilful irrelevancy;
So at last understood true nakedness
And the long debt to silence owed.

SHE LAY ALL NAKED

She lay all naked in her bed,
    And I myself lay by;
No veil but curtains about her spread,
    No covering but I:
Her head upon her shoulders seeks
    To hang in careless wise,
And full of blushes was her cheeks,
    And of wishes were her eyes.

Her blood still fresh into her face,
    As on a message came,
To say that in another place
    It meant another game;
Her cherry lip moist, plump, and fair,
    Millions of kisses crown,
Which ripe and uncropped dangled there,
    And weigh the branches down.

Her breasts, that welled so plump and high
    Bred pleasant pain in me,
For all the world I do defy
    The like felicity;
Her thighs and belly, soft and fair,
    To me were only shown:
To have seen such meat, and not to have eat,
    Would have angered any stone.

Her knees lay upward gently bent,
    And all lay hollow under,
As if on easy terms, they meant
    To fall unforced asunder;
Just so the Cyprian Queen did lie,
    Expecting in her bower;
When too long stay had kept the boy
    Beyond his promised hour.

'Dull clown,' quoth she, 'why dost delay
    Such proffered bliss to take?
Canst thou find out no other way
    Similitudes to make?'
Mad with delight I thundering
    Throw my arms about her,
But pox upon't 'twas but a dream.
    And so I lay without her.

BEFORE LOWERING THE PERFUMED CURTAIN

Before lowering the perfumed curtain to express her
     love,
She knits her eyebrows, worried that the night is too
     short.
  She urges the young lover to go to bed
First, so as to warm up the mandarin-duck quilt.

A moment later she puts down her unfinished
     needlework
And removes her silk skirt, to indulge in passion
     without end.
  Let me keep the lamp before the curtain
That I may look at her lovely face from time to time!

THE DEATH GRAPPLE

Lying between your sheets, I challenge
A watersnake in a swoln cataract
Or a starved lioness among drifts of snow.

Yet dare it out, for after each death grapple,
Each gorgon stare borrowed from very hate,
A childish innocent smile touches your lips,
Your eyelids droop, fearless and careless,
And sleep remoulds the lineaments of love.

NOW

Out of your whole life give but a moment!
All of your life that has gone before,
All to come after it, – so you ignore,
So you make perfect the present, – condense,
In a rapture of rage, for perfection's endowment,
Thought and feeling and soul and sense –
Merged in a moment which gives me at last
You around me for once, you beneath me, above me –
Me – sure that despite of time future, time past, –
This tick of our life-time's one moment you love me!
How long such suspension may linger? Ah, Sweet –
The moment eternal – just that and no more –
When ecstasy's utmost we clutch at the core
While checks burn, arms open, eyes shut and lips meet!

ROBERT BROWNING (1812–1889)   179

MEETING POINT

Time was away and somewhere else,
There were two glasses and two chairs
And two people with the one pulse
(Somebody stopped the moving stairs):
Time was away and somewhere else.

And they were neither up nor down;
The stream's music did not stop
Flowing through heather, limpid brown,
Although they sat in a coffee shop
And they were neither up nor down.

The bell was silent in the air
Holding its inverted poise –
Between the clang and clang a flower,
A brazen calyx of no noise:
The bell was silent in the air.

The camels crossed the miles of sand
That stretched around the cups and plates;
The desert was their own, they planned
To portion out the stars and dates:
The camels crossed the miles of sand.

Time was away and somewhere else.
The waiter did not come, the clock
Forgot them and the radio waltz
Came out like water from a rock:
Time was away and somewhere else.

Her fingers flicked away the ash
That bloomed again in tropic trees:
Not caring if the markets crash
When they had forests such as these,
Her fingers flicked away the ash.

God or whatever means the Good
Be praised that time can stop like this,
That what the heart has understood
Can verify in the body's peace
God or whatever means the Good.

Time was away and she was here
And life no longer what it was,
The bell was silent in the air
And all the room one glow because
Time was away and she was here.

LOUIS MACNEICE (1907–1963)   181

YOUR SHINING

Your shining – where? – rays my wide room with gold;
Grey rooms all day, green streets I visited,
Blazed with you possible; other voices bred
Yours in my quick ear; when the rain was cold
Shiver it might make shoulders I behold
Sloping through kite-slipt hours, tingling. I said
A month since, 'I will see that cloud-gold head,
Those eyes lighten, and go by': then your thunder
    rolled.

Drowned all sound else, I come driven to learn
Fearful and happy, deafening rumours of
The complete conversations of the angels, now
As nude upon some warm lawn softly turn
Toward me the silences of your breasts . . . My vow! . . .
One knee unnerves the voyeur sky enough.

THE WIFE

A frog under you,
knees drawn up
ready to leap out of time,

a dog beside you,
snuffing at you, seeking
scent of you, an idea unformulated,

I give up on
trying to answer my question,
Do I love you enough?

It's enough to be so much here. And
certainly when I catch

your mind in the
act of plucking
truth from the dark surroundingnowhere

as a swallow skims a
gnat from the
deep sky,

I don't stop to ask myself
Do I love him? but
laugh for joy.

AFTER PARADISE

Don't run anymore. Quiet. How softly it rains
On the roofs of the city. How perfect
All things are. Now, for the two of you
Waking up in a royal bed by a garret window.
For a man and a woman. For one plant divided
Into masculine and feminine which longed for each
    other.
Yes, this is my gift to you. Above ashes
On a bitter, bitter earth. Above the subterranean
Echo of clamorings and vows. So that now at dawn
You must be attentive: the tilt of a head,
A hand with a comb, two faces in a mirror
Are only forever once, even if unremembered,
So that you watch what is, though it fades away,
And are grateful every moment for your being.
Let that little park with greenish marble busts
In the pearl-gray light, under a summer drizzle,
Remain as it was when you opened the gate.
And the street of tall peeling porticoes
Which this love of yours suddenly transformed.

THE BED

The pulsing stops where time has been,
    The garden is snow-bound,
The branches weighed down and the paths filled in,
    Drifts quilt the ground.

We lie soft-caught, still now it's done,
    Loose-twined across the bed
Like wrestling statues; but it still goes on
    Inside my head.

THOM GUNN (1929–)

AT 12 O'CLOCK

At 12 o'clock in the afternoon
   in the middle of the street –
      Alexis.

Summer had all but brought the fruit
   to its perilous end:
      & the summer sun & that boy's look

did their work on me.
   Night hid the sun.
      Your face consumes my dreams.

Others feel sleep as feathered rest;
   mine but in flame refigures
      your image lit in me.

THE MORNING AFTER

The bottles are empty, the breakfast was good,
    The ladies are gay as at night;
They pull off their corsets (I knew that they would);
    I think they are just a bit tight.

The shoulders – how white! The young breasts – how
       neat!
    I stand, like the dumbest of lovers.
They throw themselves down on the bed's snowy
       sheet,
    And, giggling, dive under the covers.

They draw the bed-curtains; I watch them prepare
    To shed the last wisp of their clothing ...
And there, like the fool of the world, I stare
    At the foot of the bed, and do nothing.

HEINRICH HEINE (1797–1856),   187
TRANS. LOUIS UNTERMEYER

PENSIONNAIRES

The one was fifteen years old, the other sixteen
And they both slept in the same little room.
It happened on an oppressive September eve –
Fragile things! blue-eyed with cheeks like ivory.

To cool their frail bodies each removed
Her dainty chemise fresh with the perfume of amber.
The younger raised her hands and bent backwards,
And her sister, her hands on her breasts, kissed her.

Then fell on her knees, and, in a frenzy,
Grasped her limbs to her cheek, and her mouth
Caressed the blonde gold within the grey shadows:

And during all that time the younger counted
On her darling fingers the promised waltzes,
And, blushing, smiled innocently.

188   PAUL VERLAINE (1844–1896),
        TRANS. FRANÇOIS PIROU

TO THE FAIR CLORINDA
WHO MADE LOVE TO ME,
IMAGIN'D MORE THAN WOMAN

Fair lovely Maid, or if that Title be
Too weak, too Feminine for Nobler thee,
Permit a Name that more Approaches Truth:
And let me call thee, Lovely Charming Youth.
This last will justifie my soft complaint,
While that may serve to lessen my constraint;
And without Blushes I the Youth persue,
When so much beauteous Woman is in view.

Against thy Charms we struggle but in vain
With thy deluding Form thou giv'st us pain,
While the bright Nymph betrays us to the Swain.
In pity to our Sex sure thou wer't sent,
That we might Love, and yet be Innocent:
For sure no Crime with thee we can commit;
Of if we shou'd – thy Form excuses it.
For who, that gathers fairest Flowers believes
A Snake lies hid beneath the Fragrant Leaves.

Thou beauteous Wonder of a different kind,
Soft *Cloris* with the dear *Alexis* join'd;
When e'er the Manly part of thee, wou'd plead
Thou tempts us with the Image of the Maid,
While we the noblest Passions do extend
The Love to *Hermes*, *Aphrodite* the Friend.

THE SISTERS

After hot loveless nights, when cold winds stream
Sprinkling the frost and dew, before the light,
Bored with the foolish things that girls must dream
Because their beds are empty of delight,

Two sisters rise and strip. Out from the night
Their horses run to their low-whistled pleas –
Vast phantom shapes with eyeballs rolling white
That sneeze a fiery stream about their knees:

Through the crisp manes their stealthy prowling hands,
Stronger than curbs, in slow caresses rove,
They gallop down across the milk-white sands
And wade far out into the sleeping cove:

The frost stings sweetly with a burning kiss
As intimate as love, as cold as death:
Their lips, whereon delicious tremors hiss,
Fume with the ghostly pollen of their breath.

Far out on the grey silence of the flood
They watch the dawn in smouldering gyres expand
Beyond them; and the day burns through their blood
Like a white candle through a shuttered hand.

ROY CAMPBELL (1901–1957)   191

EPIGRAM 34

Lesbia, why are your amours
Always conducted behind open, unguarded doors?
Why do you get more excitement out of a voyeur than
    a lover?
Why is pleasure no pleasure when it's under cover?
Whores use a curtain, a bolt or a porter
To bar the public – you won't find many chinks in the
    red-light quarter.
Ask Chione or Ias how to behave:
Even the cheapest tart conceals her business inside a
    monumental grave.
If I seem too hard on you, remember my objection
Is not to fornication but detection.

SHE IS NOT SATISFIED

Outlandish idol, brown as night, who overpower
    My sense with blended musk and dry Havana,
    Work of some obi-man, some Faust of the savannah,
You witch with ebony thighs, born at the blackest
        hour,

I know Cape wine, opium, Côte de Nuits – but best I
        think
    The elixir of your mouth where love lolls, on view;
    And when the caravan of my desires sets out for you,
Your eyes are the cistern where my troubles stop and
        drink.

But pour me now from those two great dark eyes
    (Where your soul breathes) less flame, relentless
        demon:
I'm not the Styx, to give you nine embraces,

Alas! – nor, lecherous Fury, can I turn your head
    And break your last resistance by becoming
Proserpina in the Hades of your bed.

CHARLES BAUDELAIRE (1821–1867),   193
TRANS. ALISTAIR ELLIOT

MARIANA

With blackest moss the flower-plots
    Were thickly crusted, one and all:
The rusted nails fell from the knots
    That held the pear to the gable-wall.
The broken sheds looked sad and strange:
    Unlifted was the clinking latch;
    Weeded and worn the ancient thatch
Upon the lonely moated grange.
      She only said, 'My life is dreary,
        He cometh not,' she said;
      She said, 'I am aweary, aweary,
        I would that I were dead!'

Her tears fell with the dews at even;
    Her tears fell ere the dews were dried;
She could not look on the sweet heaven,
    Either at morn or eventide.
After the flitting of the bats,
    When thickest dark did trance the sky,
    She drew her casement-curtain by,
And glanced athwart the glooming flats.
      She only said, 'The night is dreary,
        He cometh not,' she said;
      She said, 'I am aweary, aweary,
        I would that I were dead!'

Upon the middle of the night,
    Waking she heard the night-fowl crow:
The cock sung out an hour ere light:
    From the dark fen the oxen's low
Came to her: without hope of change,
    In sleep she seemed to walk forlorn,
    Till cold winds woke the grey-eyed morn
About the lonely moated grange.
        She only said, 'The day is dreary,
            He cometh not,' she said;
        She said, 'I am aweary, aweary,
            I would that I were dead!'

About a stone-cast from the wall
    A sluice with blackened waters slept,
And o'er it many, round and small,
    The clustered marish-mosses crept.
Hard by a poplar shook alway,
    All silver-green with gnarlèd bark:
    For leagues no other tree did mark
The level waste, the rounding gray.
        She only said, 'My life is dreary,
            He cometh not,' she said;
        She said, 'I am aweary, aweary,
            I would that I were dead!'

And ever when the moon was low,
    And the shrill winds were up and away,
In the white curtain, to and fro,
    She saw the gusty shadow sway.
But when the moon was very low,
    And wild winds bound within their cell,
    The shadow of the poplar fell
Upon her bed, across her brow.
        She only said, 'The night is dreary,
            He cometh not,' she said;
        She said, 'I am aweary, aweary,
            I would that I were dead!'

All day within the dreamy house,
    The doors upon their hinges creaked;
The blue fly sung in the pane; the mouse
    Behind the mouldering wainscot shrieked,
Or from the crevice peered about.
    Old faces glimmered through the doors,
    Old footsteps trod the upper floors,
Old voices called her from without.
        She only said, 'My life is dreary,
            He cometh not,' she said;
        She said, 'I am aweary, aweary,
            I would that I were dead!'

196   ALFRED, LORD TENNYSON (1809–1892)

THE GIANTESS

Long, long ago, when Nature had some zest
And mothered monsters and was not effete,
I would have loved to live with a young giantess,
Like a voluptuous cat at a queen's feet.

Oh to have watched her soul begin to flower! – her size
Increasing wantonly in dreadful games;

To guess from misty looks and swimming eyes
Her heart was brooding maybe some dark flame;

To cross her magnificent contours as I pleased;

Crawl on the slope of her enormous knees;

And sometimes, when unhealthy suns had laid
Her length across the landscape, dazed with heat,
To sleep untroubled in her breasts' warm shade,
Like a calm hamlet at a mountain's feet.

CHARLES BAUDELAIRE (1821–1867),
TRANS. ALISTAIR ELLIOT

GIRL LITHE AND TAWNY

Girl lithe and tawny, the sun that forms
the fruits, that plumps the grains, that curls seaweeds
filled your body with joy, and your luminous eyes
and your mouth that has the smile of the water.

A black ravenous sun bathes you in the thread
of your black mane, when you stretch your arms.
You play with the sun as with a little brook
and it leaves you with the eyes of dark ponds.

Girl lithe and tawny, nothing draws me towards you.
Everything bears me farther away, as though you were
    noon.
You are the frenzied youth of the bee,
the drunkenness of the wave, the power of the
    wheat-ear.

My sombre heart searches for you, nevertheless,
and I love your joyful body, your slender and flowing
    voice.
Dark daisy, sweet and definitive
like the wheat-field and the sun, the poppy and the
    water.

198   PABLO NERUDA (1904–1973),
    TRANS. W. S. MERWIN

From I SING THE BODY ELECTRIC

This is the female form,
A divine nimbus exhales from it from head to foot,
It attracts with fierce undeniable attraction,
I am drawn by its breath as if I were no more than a
      helpless vapour, all falls aside but myself and it,
Books, art, religion, time, the visible and solid earth,
      and what was expected of heaven or feared of hell,
      are now consumed,
Mad filaments, ungovernable shoots play out of it, the
      response likewise ungovernable,
Ebb stung by the flow and flow stung by the ebb, love-
      flesh swelling and deliciously aching,
Limitless limpid jets of love hot and enormous,
      quivering jelly of love, white-blow and delirious
      juice,
Bridegroom night of love working surely and softly
      into the prostrate dawn,
Undulating into the willing and yielding day,
Lost in the cleave of the clasping and sweet-fleshed
      day.

This the nucleus – after the child is born of woman,
      man is born of woman,
This the bath of birth, this the merge of small and
      large, and the outlet again.

Be not ashamed women, your privilege encloses the
    rest, and is the exit of the rest,
You are the gates of the body, and you are the gates of
    the soul.

The female contains all qualities and tempers then,
She is in her place and moves with perfect balance,
She is all things duly veiled, she is both passive and
    active,
She is to conceive daughters as well as sons, and sons
    as well as daughters.

As I see my soul reflected in Nature,
As I see through a mist, One with inexpressible
    completeness, sanity, beauty,
See the bent head and arms folded over the breast, the
    Female I see.

A GLIMPSE

A glimpse through an interstice caught,
Of a crowd of workmen and drivers in a bar-room
      around the stove late of a winter night, and I
      unremark'd seated in a corner,
Of a youth who loves me and whom I love, silently
      approaching and seating himself near, that he
      may hold me by the hand,
A long while amid the noises of coming and going, of
      drinking and oath and smutty jest,
There we two, content, happy in being together,
      speaking little, perhaps not a word.

FOOT INSPECTION

The twilight barn was chinked with gleams; I saw
Soldiers with naked feet stretched on the straw,
Stiff-limbed from the long muddy march we'd done,
And ruddy-faced with April wind and sun.
With pity and stabbing tenderness I see
Those stupid, trustful eyes stare up at me.
Yet, while I stoop to Morgan's blistered toes
And ask about his boots, he never knows
How glad I'd be to die, if dying could set him free
From battles. Shyly grinning at my joke,
He pulls his grimy socks on; lights a smoke,
And thinks 'Our officer's a decent bloke'.

A BAD SLEEPER

He is a bad sleeper and it is a joy to me
To feel him well when he is the proud prey
And the strong neighbour of the best of sleep
Without false covers – no need – and without
    awakenings.
So near, so near to me that I believe he enflames me
In some way, with his overwhelming desire, that I feel
In my ravished and trembling body.
If we find ourselves face to face, and if he turns
Close to my side, as lovers are wont to do,
His haunches, deliriously dreamy or not,
Sudden, mutinous, malicious, stubborn, whorish,
In the name-of-God, his cravings, so gentle, will pierce
    my flesh,
And leave me girdled like a eunuch,
Or if I should turn to him with the wish
To soothe him; or, if peacefully we lie, his quietness,
Brutal and gentle, will suffuse my body in his;
And my spirit, out of happiness, will submerge and
    overwhelm him,
And prostrate him, infinite in that tack.
Am I happy? Totus in benigno positus!

PAUL VERLAINE (1844–1896),
TRANS. FRANÇOIS PIROU

DAYS OF 1901

This he had in him that set him apart,
that in spite of all his dissoluteness
and his great experience in love,
despite the habitual harmony
that existed between his attitude and his age
there happened to be moments – however,
rarest moments, to be sure – when he gave the
impression of a flesh almost untouched.

The beauty of his twenty-nine years,
so tested by sensual delight,
at moments paradoxically recalled
a young man who – rather gawkily – surrenders
his pure body to love for the very first time.

C. P. CAVAFY (1863–1933),
TRANS. RAE DALVEN

O TAN-FACED PRAIRIE-BOY

O tan-faced prairie-boy,
Before you came to camp came many a welcome gift,
Praises and presents came and nourishing food, till at
    last among the recruits,
You came, taciturn, with nothing to give – we but
    look'd on each other,
When lo! more than all the gifts of the world you gave
    me.

THE BEAUTIFUL SWIMMER

I see a beautiful gigantic swimmer swimming naked
    through the eddies of the sea,
His brown hair lies close and even to his head, he
    strikes out with courageous arms, he urges
    himself with his legs,
I see his white body, I see his undaunted eyes,
I hate the swift-running eddies that would dash him
    head-foremost on the rocks.

What are you doing you ruffianly red-trickled waves?
Will you kill the courageous giant? will you kill him in
    the prime of his middle-age?

Steady and long he struggles,
He is baffled, bang'd, bruis'd, he holds out while his
    strength holds out,
The slapping eddies are spotted with his blood, they
    bear him away, they roll him, swing him, turn
    him,
His beautiful body is borne in the circling eddies, it is
    continually bruis'd on rocks,
Swiftly and out of sight is borne the brave corpse.

A THOUSAND AND THREE

My lovers come, not from the floating classes: they're
Labourers from the depths of suburbs or the land,
Aged fifteen, twenty, with no graces, but an air
Of pretty brutal strength and manners none too grand.

I like them in their work-clothes – jacket, overalls:
Smelling of pure and simple health, never a whiff
Of scent: their step sounds heavy, yes, but still it falls
Nimble enough – they're young, their bounce a little stiff.

Their crafty and wide eyes crackle with cordial
Mischief: the wit of their naïvely knowing quips
Comes salted with gay swearwords, to be rhythmical,
From their fresh, wholesome mouths and soundly
    kissing lips;

With energetic knobs and buttockfuls of joy
They can rejoice my arsehole and my cock all night;
By lamplight and at dawn their flesh, all over joy,
Wakes my desire again, tired but still full of fight.

Thighs, hands, and souls, all of me mixed up, memory,
     feet,
Heart, back and ear and nose and all my ringing guts
Begin to bawl in chorus as they hit the beat,
Reeling and jig-a-jigging in their frenzied ruts:

A crazy dance, a crazy chorus as we're lined
Up, up, divinely rising because hell is high
On heavenly routes: I dance to save myself, and find,
Swimming in sweat, it's in our common breath I fly.

So, my two Charleses: one, young tiger with cat's eyes,
A choirboy with his volume swelling rough and thick;
The other a wild blade so cheeky I surprise
Him only with my dizzy penchant for his prick;

And Odilon, a kid, equipped, though, like a lord:
His feet in love with mine, which rave about their
     catch –
Those toes! – though thick and fast the rest of him's
     adored –
Those feet! – there's nothing like them! – even they
     don't match!

How they caress, so satin cool, with sensitive
Knuckles that stroke the soles and, round the ankles,
    graze
Over the veiny arch! how these strange kisses give
A sweet soul to this quadruped with soulful ways!

Then Antoine, with that tail of legendary size,
My god, my phallocrat who triumphs from the rear,
Piercing my heart with the blue lightning of his eyes,
My violet arsehole with his terrifying spear;

Paul, a blond athlete – pectorals that you could eat! –
A white breast with hard buttons that are sucked as
    much
As the more juicy end; and François, lithe as wheat,
His pecker coiled in that fantastic dancer's crutch;

Auguste, who daily makes himself more masculine
(Oh when it happened first he was a pretty lass!);
Jules, rather whorish with his pallid beauty's skin;
Henri, the marvellous conscript who's gone off, alas! –

I see you all, alone or friends together, some
Unique, some I confuse, a vision of past love
Clear as my passions who come now, or are to come,
My countless darlings who can never come enough!

PAUL VERLAINE (1844–1896),
TRANS. ALISTAIR ELLIOT

Far from the tender Tribe of Boys remove,
For they've a thousand ways to kindle Love.
This, pleases as he strides the manag'd Horse,
And holds the taughten'd Rein with early Force;
This, as he swims, delights the Fancy best,
Raising the smiling Wave with snowy Breast:
This, with a comely Look and manly Airs;
And that with Virgin Modesty ensnares.
But if at first you find him not inclin'd
To Love, have Patience, Time will change his Mind.

*

And you, whate'er your Fav'rite does, approve,
For Condescension leads the Way to love.
Go with him where he goes, tho' long the Way,
And the fierce Dog-star fires the sultry Way;
Or the gay Rainbow girds the bluish Sky,
And threatens rattling Show'rs of Rain are nigh.
If sailing on the Water be his Will,
Then steer the Wherry with a dext'rous Skill:
Nor think it hard Fatigues and Pains to bear,
But still be ready with a willing Cheer.
If he'll inclose the Vales for savage Spoils,
Then on thy Shoulders bear the Nets and Toils;
If Fencing be the Fav'rite Sport he'll use,

Take up the Files, and artlessly oppose;
Seem as intent, yet oft expose your Breast,
Neglect your Guard, and let him get the best;
Then he'll be mild, then you a Kiss may seize,
He'll struggle, but at length comply with ease;
Reluctant, tho' at first you'll find him grow
Ev'n fond, when round your Neck his Arms he'll
    throw.

AURELIUS

Aurelius, I'm entrusting you with all
I love most, with my boy. I ask a small
Favour. If you have ever pledged your soul
To keep some cherished object pure and whole,
Then guard him – I don't mean from any stranger
Walking the streets on business bent: the danger
I fear is you yourself and that great spike
That ruins good and naughty boys alike.
When you're outside the house, wave your erection
At any one you like, in what direction
You please, but (I'm not asking much, I trust)
Make him the one exception. If, though, lust
And sheer perversity unhinge your reason
And drive you to the abominable treason
Of plotting against me, a grisly fate
Awaits you. Feet chained, through the open gate
Of your own flesh you'll suffer, for your sins,
The thrust of radishes and mullets' fins.

IN DESPAIR

He has lost him completely.   And now he is seeking
on the lips of   every new lover
the lips of his beloved;   in the embrace
of every new lover   he seeks to be deluded
that he is the same lad,   that it is to him he is yielding.

He has lost him completely,   as if he had never been at
    all.
For he wanted – so he said –   he wanted to be saved
from the stigmatized,   the sick sensual delight;
from the stigmatized,   sensual delight of shame.
There was still time –   as he said – to be saved.

He has lost him completely,   as if he had never been at
    all.
In his imagination,   in his delusions,
on the lips of others   it is his lips he is seeking;
he is longing to feel again   the love he has known.

C. P. CAVAFY (1863–1933), TRANS. RAE DALVEN   213

SURPRISE, SURPRISE

Nizam the pederast, whose delight in boys
Was known throughout Bagdad, one afternoon
In a secluded place saw in a clearing
The flash of limbs behind a nearby bush,
And looking closer came upon a youth
Who seemed more lovely than his dreams had
    promised,
Lying asleep in shade, his head pressed deep
Into crossed arms, his long slim body
Quite naked, the firm buttocks firmly offered.
Quick as a jackal pouncing, Nizam jumped
Upon the lad, his robe about his waist,
The startled boy pierced by his lusty cock
Before you could say knife. Not until later,
When boy lay panting on the flattened grass,
Did Nizam, pausing to embrace his love,
Discover him a her, surprised but pleased
At being given such pleasure at a source
No previous lover seemed to know about.

Nizam converted? Never. But the girl
Now gives her lovers strange instruction.

214   ANON (9TH CENTURY ARABIC),
       TRANS. DEREK PARKER

HELLO THERE

– Hello there. – *Hello there yourself.*
– What's your name? – *What's yours?*
– Let's not get too involved right away.
– *Let's not.* – Are you busy?
– *I have my full-time admirers.*
– Like to have dinner with me?
– *If you like.* – Splendid. How much
does it come to? – *Nothing fixed in advance.*
– How exotic! – *After you've had me in bed,*
it's up to you what you give.
– Fair enough! What's your address?
I'll call for you. – *You look it up.*
– When can you make it? – *Whenever you want.*
– I want to right now. – *Lead the way.*

PHILODEMUS (110–30 BC),   215
TRANS. WILLIAM MOEBIUS

THE MORAL TAXI RIDE

They found a taxi. He took her home.
She spoke of her husband the while.
He knew she had power to charm him, some.
He didn't as much as smile.

They rode down the midnight thoroughfare.
While somebody sat at the wheel.
The stars had painted their faces fair.
The streets were empty and still.

And when the taxi swung around curves,
Their knees just managed to touch.
And it was plainly a case of nerves,
Whenever it swung too much.

He recommended a show to see.
His manner was slightly forced.
She spoke of her lovely family.
Her voice sounded thin and lost.

And though he looked out of the window, he knew
That the gaze she gave him was steady.
And she was suddenly troubled too,
And thought, "We are there already."

Then both of them didn't speak for a space.
Above them, some lightning broke.
The thing was awkward. He felt that the place
Was right for a funny joke.

The air was mild. And the taxi ran.
It galloped on faith and fuel.
They didn't think Nature could do them a damn,
But rubbing knees was cruel.

So at last they got out. He gave her his hand.
And went. And left it at that.
Though later, at home in his room, he would stand
And kick a hole in his hat.

ERICH KÄSTNER (1899–   ),   217
TRANS. J. D. ROTHENBERG

CARMINA, V: TO CELIA

Come my Celia, let us prove,
While we may, the sports of love;
Time will not be ours, for ever:
He, at length, our good will sever.
Spend not then his guifts in vaine.
Sunnes, that set, may rise againe:
But if once we loose this light,
'Tis, with us, perpetuall night.
Why should we deferre our joyes?
Fame, and rumor are but toyes.
Cannot we delude the eyes
Of a few poore household spyes?
Or his easier eares beguile,
So removed by our wile?
'Tis no sinne, loves fruit to steale,
But the sweet theft to reveale:
To be taken, to be seene,
These have crimes accounted beene.

CATULLUS (*c.* 84–*c.* 54 BC),
TRANS. BEN JONSON

NOTHING TO FEAR

All fixed: early arrival at the flat
Lent by a friend, whose note says *Lucky sod*;
Drinks on the tray; the cover-story pat
And quite uncheckable; her husband off
Somewhere with all the kids till six o'clock
(Which ought to be quite long enough):
And all worth while: face really beautiful,
Good legs and hips, and as for breasts – my God.
What about guilt, compunction and such stuff?
I've had my fill of all that cock;
It'll wear off, as usual.

Yes, all fixed. Then why this slight trembling,
Dry mouth, quick pulse-rate, sweaty hands,
As though she were the first? No, not impatience,
Nor fear of failure, thank you, Jack.
Beauty, they tell me, is a dangerous thing,
Whose touch will burn, but I'm asbestos, see?
All worth while – it's a dead coincidence
That sitting here, a bag of glands
Tuned up to concert pitch, I seem to sense
A different style of caller at my back,
As cold as ice, but just as set on me.

KINGSLEY AMIS (1922–   )   219

CARNAL KNOWLEDGE

Even in bed I pose: desire may grow
More circumstantial and less circumspect
Each night, but an acute girl would suspect
My thoughts might not be, like my body, bare.
I wonder if you know, or, knowing care?
You know I know you know I know you know.

I am not what I seem, believe me, so
For the magnanimous pagan I pretend
Substitute a forked creature as your friend.
When darkness lies – without a roll or stir –
Flaccid, you want a competent poseur
Whose seeming is the only thing to know.

I prod you, you react. Thus to and fro
We turn, to see ourselves perform the same
Comical act inside the tragic game.
Or is it perhaps simpler: could it be
A mere tear-jerker void of honesty
In which there are no motives left to know?

Lie back. Within a minute I will stow
Your greedy mouth, but will not yet to grips.
'There is a space between the breast and lips.'
Also a space between the thighs and head,
So great, we might as well not be in bed:
For we learn nothing here we did not know.

I hardly hoped for happy thoughts, although
In a most happy sleeping time I dreamt
We did not hold each other in contempt.
Then lifting from my lids night's penny weights
I saw that lack of love contaminates.
You know I know you know I know you know.

Abandon me to stammering, and go;
If you have tears, prepare to cry elsewhere –
I know of no emotion we can share.
Your intellectual protests are a bore,
And even now I pose, so now go, for
I know you know.

THOM GUNN (1929–   )   221

LATE-FLOWERING LUST

My head is bald, my breath is bad,
    Unshaven is my chin,
I have not now the joys I had
    When I was young in sin.

I run my fingers down your dress
    With brandy-certain aim
And you respond to my caress
    And maybe feel the same.

But I've a picture of my own
    On this reunion night,
Wherein two skeletons are shewn
    To hold each other tight;

Dark sockets look on emptiness
    Which once was loving-eyed,
The mouth that opens for a kiss
    Has got no tongue inside.

I cling to you inflamed with fear
    As now you cling to me,
I feel how frail you are my dear
    And wonder what will be –

A week? or twenty years remain?
    And then – what kind of death?
A losing fight with frightful pain
    Or a gasping fight for breath?

Too long we let our bodies cling,
    We cannot hide disgust
At all the thoughts that in us spring
    From this late-flowering lust.

GOOD GOD, WHAT A NIGHT THAT WAS

Good God, what a night that was,
The bed was so soft, and how we clung,
Burning together, lying this way and that,
Our uncontrollable passions
Flowing through our mouths.
If I could only die that way,
I'd say goodbye to the business of living.

PARODY OF A LOVER

Sweethearts, we felt the same pleasure,
So deeply were we involved.
You sensed my desire,
And I guessed your heart.

Serene years went by
Harmonious as lute and harp.
Good times did not keep me company,
Midway we grew distant like Antares and Orion.
You separated south of northern hills,
I separated south of south river.
Happy joy no longer sought,
Heavy thoughts, how to bear them?

My eyes carry the charm of your image fair,
My ears hold the beauty of your clear voice.
Through the day endless memories surge,
Far into night I sigh in lonely grief.

When you departed on circuit
And said we must part, tears soaked my collar.
Please honour me with your jade footsteps,
One look is more than a thousand in gold.

LI CH'UNG (*b.* AD 323), TRANS. ANNE BIRRELL   225

ACT OF LOVE

This is not the man that women choose,
This honest fellow, stuffed to the lips with groans,
Whose passion cannot even speak plain prose
But grunts and mumbles in the muddiest tones.
His antics are disgusting or absurd,
His lust obtrusive, craning from its nest
At awkward times its blind reptilian head;
His jealousy and candour are a pest.

Now, here is the boy that women will lie down for:
The snappy actor, skilled in the lover's part,
A lyric fibber and subvocal tenor
Whose pleasure in the play conceals his art;
Who, even as he enters her warm yes,
Hears fluttering hands and programmes in the vast
Auditorium beyond her voice
Applauding just one member of the cast.

THE IMPERFECT ENJOYMENT

Naked she lay, clasped in my longing arms,
I filled with love, and she all over charms;
Both equally inspired with eager fire,
Melting through kindness, flaming in desire.
With arms, legs, lips, close clinging to embrace,
She clips me to her breast and sucks me to her face.
Her nimble tongue, Love's lesser lightning, played
Within my mouth, and to my thoughts conveyed
Swift orders that I should prepare to throw
The all-dissolving thunderbolt below.
My fluttering soul, sprung with the pointed kiss,
Hangs hovering o'er her balmy brinks of bliss.
But whilst her busy hand would guide that part
Which should convey my soul up to her heart,
In liquid raptures I dissolve all o'er,
Melt into sperm, and spend at every pore.
A touch from any part of her had done't –
Her hand, her foot, her very look's a cunt.

    Smiling, she chides in a kind murmuring noise
And from her body wipes the clammy joys,
When with a thousand kisses wandering o'er
My panting bosom, 'Is there then no more?'
She cries. 'All this to love and rapture's due;
Must we not pay a debt to pleasure, too?'

But I, the most forlorn, lost man alive
To show my wished obedience vainly strive.
I sigh, alas!, and kiss – but cannot swive.
Eager desires confound my first intent,
Succeeding shame does more success prevent,
And rage at last confirms me impotent.
Even her fair hand, which might bid heat return
To frozen age, and make cold hermits burn,
Applied to my dead cinder warms no more
Than fire to ashes could past flames restore.
Trembling, confused, despairing, limber, dry,
A wishing, weak, unmoving lump I lie.
This dart of love whose piercing point, oft tried,
With virgin blood ten thousand maids has dyed,
Which nature still directed with such art
That it through every cunt reached every heart
(Stiffly resolved, 'twould carelessly invade
Woman or man, nor aught its fury stayed –
Where'er it pierced, a cunt it found or made)
Now languid lies in this unhappy hour
Shrunk up and sapless like a withered flower.

Thou treacherous, base deserter of my flame,
False to my passion, fatal to my fame,
Through what mistaken magic dost thou prove
So true to lewdness, so untrue to love?
What oyster- cinder- beggar- common whore

Didst thou e'er fail in all thy life before?
When vice, disease and scandal lead the way
With what officious haste dost thou obey!
Like a rude, roaring hector in the streets
Who scuffles, cuffs and jostles all he meets,
But if his King or country claim his aid
The rake-hell villain shrinks and hides his head;
Even so thy brutal valour is displayed,
Breaks every stew, does each small whore invade,
But when great Love the onset does command,
Base recreant to thy prince, thou darest not stand.
Worse part of me, and henceforth hated most,
Through all the town a common fucking post
On whom each whore relieves her tingling cunt
As hogs on gates do rub themselves and grunt:
Mayst thou to ravenous cankers be a prey,
Or in consuming weepings waste away;
May stranguary and stone thy days attend,
Mayst thou ne'er piss who didst refuse to spend
When all my joys did on false thee depend.
And may ten thousand abler pricks agree
To do the wronged Corinna right for thee.

LORD ROCHESTER (1647–1680)   229

From THE RAPE OF LUCRECE

Her lily hand her rosy cheek lies under,
Cozening the pillow of a lawful kiss;
Who, therefore angry, seems to part in sunder,
Swelling on either side to want his bliss;
Between whose hills her head entombed is;
    Where like a virtuous monument she lies,
    To be admired of lewd unhallowed eyes.

Without the bed her other fair hand was,
On the green coverlet, whose perfect white
Showed like an April daisy on the grass,
With pearly sweat resembling dew of night.
Her eyes, like marigolds, had sheathed their light,
    And canopied in darkness sweetly lay
    Till they might open to adorn the day.

Her hair like golden threads played with her breath –
O modest wantons, wanton modesty!
Showing life's triumph in the map of death,
And death's dim look in life's mortality.
Each in her sleep themselves so beautify
    As if between them twain there were no strife,
    But that life lived in death, and death in life.

Her breasts like ivory globes circled with blue,
A pair of maiden worlds unconquerèd,
Save of their lord no bearing yoke they knew,
And him by oath they truly honourèd.
These worlds in Tarquin new ambition bred,
    Who like a foul usurper went about
    From this fair throne to heave the owner out.

What could he see but mightily he noted?
What did he note but strongly he desired?
What he beheld, on that he firmly doted,
And in his will his willful eye he tired.
With more than admiration he admired
    Her azure veins, her alabaster skin,
    Her coral lips, her snow-white dimpled chin.

As the grim lion fawneth o'er his prey
Sharp hunger by the conquest satisfied,
So o'er this sleeping soul doth Tarquin stay,
His rage of lust by gazing qualified;
Slacked, not suppressed; for, standing by her side,
    His eye, which late this mutiny restrains,
    Unto a greater uproar tempts his veins.

And they, like straggling slaves for pillage fighting,
Obdurate vassals fell exploits effecting,
In bloody death and ravishment delighting,
Nor children's tears nor mothers' groans respecting,
Swell in their pride, the onset still expecting.
    Anon his beating heart, alarum striking,
    Gives the hot charge and bids them do their liking.

His drumming heart cheers up his burning eye,
His eye commends the leading to his hand;
His hand, as proud of such a dignity,
Smoking with pride, marched on to make his stand
On her bare breast, the heart of all her land,
    Whose ranks of blue veins, as his hand did scale,
    Left their round turrets destitute and pale.

They, mustering to the quiet cabinet
Where their dear governess and lady lies,
Do tell her she is dreadfully beset
And fright her with confusion of their cries.
She, much amazed, breaks ope her locked-up eyes,
    Who, peeping forth this tumult to behold,
    Are by his flaming torch dimmed and controlled.

Imagine her as one in dead of night
From forth dull sleep by dreadful fancy waking,
That thinks she hath beheld some ghastly sprite,
Whose grim aspect sets every joint a-shaking.
What terror 'tis! but she, in worser taking,
　　From sleep disturbèd, heedfully doth view
　　The sight which makes supposèd terror true.

Wrapped and confounded in a thousand fears,
Like to a new-killed bird she trembling lies.
She dares not look; yet, winking, there appears
Quick-shifting antics ugly in her eyes.
Such shadows are the weak brain's forgeries,
　　Who, angry that the eyes fly from their lights,
　　In darkness daunts them with more dreadful sights.

His hand, that yet remains upon her breast
(Rude ram, to batter such an ivory wall!)
May feel her heart (poor citizen) distressed,
Wounding itself to death, rise up and fall,
Beating her bulk, that his hand shakes withal.
　　This moves in him more rage and lesser pity,
　　To make the breach and enter this sweet city.

THE SICK ROSE

O Rose, thou art sick!
The invisible worm
That flies in the night,
In the howling storm,

Has found out thy bed
Of crimson joy:
And his dark secret love
Does thy life destroy.

WILLIAM BLAKE (1757–1827)

A TRUE MAID

No, no; for my virginity,
    When I lose that, says Rose, I'll die:
Behind the elms, last night, cried Dick,
    Rose, were you not extremely sick?

MATTHEW PRIOR (1664–1721)

THE RAM

He jangles his keys in the rain
and I follow like a lamb.
His house is as smoky as a dive.
We go straight downstairs to his room.

I lie on his bed and watch him
undress. His orange baseball jacket,
all the way from Ontario,
drops to the floor – THE RAMS, in felt,

arched across the hunky back.
He unzips his calf-length
Star-walkers, his damp black Levi's
and adjusts his loaded modelling-pouch:

he stands before me in his socks –
as white as bridesmaids,
little daisies, driven snow.
John Wayne watches from the wall

beside a shelf-ful of pistols.
Well, he says, *d'you like it?*
All I can think of is Granny,
how she used to shake her head,

when I stood by her bed on Sundays,
so proud in my soap-smelling
special frock, and say *Ah*,
Bless your little cotton socks!

THE GERANIUM

In the close covert of a grove
By nature formed for scenes of love,
Said Susan in a lucky hour:
'Observe yon sweet geranium flower.
How straight upon its stalk it stands,
And tempts our violating hands,
Whilst the soft bud, as yet unspread,
Hangs down its pale declining head.
Yet soon as it is ripe to blow,
The stems shall rise, the head shall glow.'
'Nature,' said I, 'my lovely Sue,
To all her followers lends a clue.
Her simple laws themselves explain
As links of one continued chain;
For her the mysteries of creation
Are but the works of generation.
Yon blushing, strong, triumphant flower
Is in the crisis of its power;
But short, alas, its vigorous reign;
He sheds his seed, and drops again.
The bud that hangs in pale decay
Feels not, as yet, the plastic ray.
Tomorrow's sun shall make him rise,
Then, too, he sheds his seed, and dies.
But words, my love, are vain and weak;

For proof, let bright example speak.'
Then straight before the wondering maid
The tree of life I gently laid.
'Observe, sweet Sue, his drooping head,
How pale, how languid, and how dead.
Yet let the sun of thy bright eyes
Shine but a moment, it shall rise.
Let but the dew of thy soft hand
Refresh the stem, it straight shall stand.
Already, see, it swells, it grows,
Its head is redder than the rose,
Its shrivelled fruit, of dusky hue,
Now glows – a present fit for Sue.
The balm of life each artery fills,
And in o'erflowing drops distils.'
'Oh, me!' cried Susan, 'When is this?
What strange tumultuous throbs of bliss!
Sure, never mortal till this hour
Felt such emotion at a flower!
Oh, serpent, cunning to deceive,
Sure 'tis this tree that tempted Eve.
The crimson apples hang so fair
Alas! what woman could forbear?'
'Well hast thou guessed, my love,' I cried,
'It is the tree by which she died –
The tree which could content her.
All nature, Susan, seeks the centre.

Yet let us still poor Eve forgive,
It's the tree by which we live.
For lovely women still it grows,
And in the centre only blows.
But chief for thee it spreads its charms,
For paradise is in thy arms . . .'
I ceased, for nature kindly here
Began to whisper in her ear,
And lovely Sue lay softly panting
While the geranium tree was planting,
'Till in the heat of amorous strife
She burst the mellow tree of life.
'Oh, heaven!' cried Susan with a sigh,
'The hour we taste – we surely die.
Strange raptures seize my fainting frame,
And all my body glows with flame.
Yet let me snatch one parting kiss
To tell my love I die with bliss –
That pleased thy Susan yields her breath;
Oh, who would live, if this be death?'

THE BALLAD OF VILLON AND FAT MADGE

"'Tis no sin for a man to labour in his vocation.'
'The night cometh, when no man can work.'

What though the beauty I love and serve be cheap,
    Ought you to take me for a beast or fool?
All things a man could wish are in her keep;
    For her I turn swashbuckler in love's school.
    When folk drop in, I take my pot and stool
And fall to drinking with no more ado.
I fetch them bread, fruit, cheese, and water, too;
    I say all's right so long as I'm well paid;
'Look in again when your flesh troubles you,
    Inside this brothel where we drive our trade.'

But soon the devil's among us flesh and fell,
    When penniless to bed comes Madge my whore;
I loathe the very sight of her like hell.
    I snatch gown, girdle, surcoat, all she wore,
    And tell her, these shall stand against her score.
She grips her hips with both hands, cursing God,
Swearing by Jesus' body, bones, and blood,
    That they shall not. Then I, no whit dismayed,
Cross her cracked nose with some stray shiver of wood
    Inside this brothel where we drive our trade.

When all's up she drops me a windy word,
    Bloat like a beetle puffed and poisonous:
Grins, thumps my pate, and calls me dickey-bird,
    And cuffs me with a fist that's ponderous.
    We sleep like logs, being drunken both of us;
Then when we wake her womb begins to stir;
To save her seed she gets me under her
    Wheezing and whining, flat as planks are laid:
And thus she spoils me for a whoremonger
    Inside this brothel where we drive our trade.

Blow, hail or freeze, I've bread here baked rent free!
Whoring's my trade, and my whore pleases me;
    Bad cat, bad rat; we're just the same if weighed.
We that love filth, filth follows us, you see;
Honour flies from us, as from her we flee
    Inside this brothel where we drive our trade.

    I bequeath likewise to fat Madge
        This little song to learn and study;
    By God's head she's a sweet fat fadge,
        Devout and soft of flesh and ruddy;
    I love her with my soul and body,
    So doth she me, sweet dainty thing.
        If you fall in with such a lady,
    Read it, and give it her to sing.

FRANÇOIS VILLON (1431–AFTER 1463),   241
TRANS. A. C. SWINBURNE

EITHER SHE WAS FOUL

Either she was foul, or her attire was bad,
Or she was not the wench I wished t'have had.
Idly I lay with her, as if I loved not,
And like a burden grieved the bed that moved not.
Yet though both of us performed our true intent,
Yet could I not cast anchor where I meant.
She on my neck her ivory arms did throw,
Her arms far whiter than the Scythian snow.
And eagerly she kissed me with her tongue,
And under mine her wanton thigh she flung.
Yea, and she soothed me up and called me sire,
And used all speech that might provoke and stir.
Yet, like as if cold hemlock I had drunk,
It mockèd me, hung down the head, and sunk.
Like a dull cipher or rude block I lay,
Or shade or body was I, who can say?
What will my age do, age I cannot shun,
When in my prime my force is spent and done?
I blush, that being youthful, hot and lusty,
I prove neither youth nor man, but old and rusty.
Pure rose she, like a nun to sacrifice,
Or one that with her tender brother lies.
Yet boarded I the golden Chie twice,
And Libas, and the white-cheeked Pitho thrice.
Corinna craved it in a summer's night,

242

And nine sweet bouts we had before daylight.
What, waste my limbs through some Thessalian
    charms?
May spells and drugs do silly souls such harms?
With virgin wax hath some imbaste my joints
And pierced my liver with sharp needles' points?
Charms change corn to grass and make it die.
By charms are running springs and fountains dry.
By charms mast crops from oaks, from vines grapes fall,
And fruit from trees when there's no wind at all.
Why might not then my sinews be enchanted,
And I grow faint, as with some spirit haunted?
To this add shame: shame to perform it quailed me
And was the second cause why vigour failed me.
My idle thoughts delighted her no more
Than did the robe or garment which she wore.
Yet might her touch make youthful Pylius fire
And Tithon livelier than his years require.
Even her I had, and she had me in vain;
What might I crave more if I asked again?
I think the great gods grieved they had bestowed
The benefit which lewdly I for-slowed.
I wished to be received in. In I get me
To kiss. I kiss. To lie with her, she let me.
Why was I blessed? Why made king to refuse it?
Chuff-like had I not gold and could not use it?
So in a spring thrives he that told so much,

243

And looks upon the fruits he cannot touch.
Hath any rose so from a fresh young maid,
As she might straight have gone to church and prayed?
Well I believe she kissed not as she should,
Nor used the sleight and cunning which she could.
Huge oaks, hard adamants might she have moved,
And with sweet words cause deaf rocks to have loved.
Worthy she was to move both gods and men,
But neither was I man, nor lived then.
Can deaf ear take delight when Phaemius sings?
Or Thamiras in curious painted things?
What sweet thought is there but I had the same?
And one gave place still as another came.
Yet, nonwithstanding, like one dead it lay,
Drooping more than a rose pulled yesterday.
Now, when he should not jet, he bolts upright
And craves his task, and seeks to be at fight.
Lie down with shame, and see thou stir no more,
Seeing thou wouldst deceive me as before.
Thou cozenest me, by thee surprised am I,
And bide sore loss with endless infamy.
Nay more, the wench did not disdain a whit
To take it in her hand and play with it.
But when she saw it would by no means stand,
But still drooped down, regarding not her hand,
'Why mockst thou me?' she cried. 'Or, being ill,
Who bade thee lie down here against thy will?

Either thou art witch, with blood of frogs new dead,
Or jaded camest thou from some other bed.'
With that, her loose gown on, from me she cast her –
In skipping out her naked feet much graced her.
And, lest her maid should know of this disgrace,
To cover it, spilt water on the place.

PORPHYRIA'S LOVER

The rain set early in to-night,
　　The sullen wind was soon awake,
It tore the elm-tops down for spite,
　　And did its worst to vex the lake:
　　I listened with heart fit to break.
When glided in Porphyria; straight
　　She shut the cold out and the storm,
And kneeled and made the cheerless grate
　　Blaze up, and all the cottage warm;
　　Which done, she rose, and from her form
Withdrew the dripping cloak and shawl,
　　And laid her soiled gloves by, untied
Her hat and let the damp hair fall,
　　And, last, she sat down by my side
　　And called me. When no voice replied,
She put my arm about her waist,
　　And made her smooth white shoulder bare,
And all her yellow hair displaced,
　　And, stooping, made my cheek lie there,
　　And spread, o'er all, her yellow hair,
Murmuring how she loved me – she
　　Too weak, for all her heart's endeavour,
To set its struggling passion free
　　From pride, and vainer ties dissever,
　　And give herself to me for ever.

But passion sometimes would prevail,
    Nor could to-night's gay feast restrain
A sudden thought of one so pale
    For love of her, and all in vain:
    So, she was come through wind and rain.
Be sure I looked up at her eyes
    Happy and proud; at last I knew
Porphyria worshipped me; surprise
    Made my heart swell, and still it grew
    While I debated what to do.
That moment she was mine, mine, fair,
    Perfectly pure and good: I found
A thing to do, and all her hair
    In one long yellow string I wound
    Three times her little throat around,
And strangled her. No pain felt she;
    I am quite sure she felt no pain.
As a shut bud that holds a bee,
    I warily oped her lids: again
    Laughed the blue eyes without a stain.
And I untightened next the tress
    About her neck; her cheek once more
Blushed bright beneath my burning kiss:
    I propped her head up as before,
    Only, this time my shoulder bore
Her head, which droops upon it still:
    The smiling rosy little head,

So glad it has its utmost will,
    That all it scorned at once is fled,
    And I, its love, am gained instead!
Porphyria's love: she guessed not how
    Her darling one wish would be heard.
And thus we sit together now,
    And all night long we have not stirred,
    And yet God has not said a word!

SAD LOVE

The moon spits fire,
Lotuses droop
And loaded with fragrance
Mingle in sad love.
Kokila, bird of spring,
Why do you torture?
Why do you sing
Your love-provoking song?
My lover is not here
And yet the god of love
Schemes on and on.
You do not know the meaning of 'tomorrow'.
'Tomorrow' is *my* tomorrow
And water
Escapes the dam of youth.
You are in love,
So is your lover,
And your two banks
Are brimming with the flood.
My lover left and I would die
Than wait still longer
For his loved return.

The fragrance of flowers
Enters the city,
Bees sing,
The moon and night enchant,
Yet all are enemies.

ODE 487

With last night's wine still singing in my head,
I sought the tavern at the break of day,
Though half the world was still asleep in bed;
The harp and flute were up and in full swing,
And a most pleasant morning sound made they;
Already was the wine-cup on the wing.
'Reason,' said I, ''t is past the time to start,
If you would reach your daily destination,
The holy city of intoxication.'
So did I pack him off, and he depart
With a stout flask for fellow-traveller.

Left to myself, the tavern-wench I spied,
And sought to win her love by speaking fair;
Alas! she turned upon me, scornful-eyed,
And mocked my foolish hopes of winning her.
Said she, her arching eyebrows like a bow:
'Thou mark for all the shafts of evil tongues!
Thou shalt not round my middle clasp me so,
Like my good girdle – not for all thy songs! –
So long as thou in all created things
Seest but thyself the centre and the end.
Go spread thy dainty nets for other wings –
Too high the Anca's nest for thee, my friend.'

Then took I shelter from that stormy sea
In the good ark of wine; yet, woe is me!
Saki and comrade and minstrel all by turns,
She is of maidens the compendium
Who my poor heart in such a fashion spurns.
Self, HAFIZ, self! That must thou overcome!
Hearken the wisdom of the tavern-daughter!
Vain little baggage – well, upon my word!
Thou fairy figment made of clay and water,
As busy with thy beauty as a bird.

Well, HAFIZ, Life's a riddle – give it up:
There is no answer to it but this cup.

HAFIZ (*d. c.* 1390),
TRANS. RICHARD LE GALLIENNE

FOLK TUNE

It's not that the Muse feels like clamming up,
it's more like high time for the lad's last nap.
And the scarf-waving lass who wished him the best
drives a steamroller across his chest.

And the words won't rise either like that rod
or like logs to rejoin their old grove's sweet rot,
and, like eggs in the frying pan, the face
spills its eyes all over the pillowcase.

Are you warm tonight under those six veils
in that basin of yours whose strung bottom wails;
where like fish that gasp at the foreign blue
my raw lip was catching what then meant you?

I would have hare's ears sewn to my bald head,
in thick woods for your sake I'd gulp drops of lead,
and from black gnarled snags in the oil-smooth pond
I'd bob up to your face as some *Tirpitz* won't.

But it's not on the cards or the waiter's tray,
and it pains to say where one's hair turns gray.
There are more blue veins than the blood to swell
their dried web, let alone some remote brain cell.

We are parting for good, little friend, that's that.
Draw an empty circle on your yellow pad.
This will be me: no insides in thrall.
Stare at it a while, then erase the scrawl.

FEVER

Impatient all the foggy day for night
  You plunged into the bar eager to loot.
A self-defeating eagerness: you're light,
  You change direction and shift from foot to foot,
Too skittish to be capable of repose
  Or of deciding what is worth pursuit.

Your mother thought you beautiful, I suppose,
  She dandled you all day and watched your sleep.
Perhaps that's half the trouble. And it grows:
  An unattended conqueror now, you keep
Getting less beautiful toward the evening's end.
  The boy's potential sours to malice, deep
Most against those who've done nothing to offend.
  They did not notice you, and only I
Have watched you much – though not as covert friend
  But picturing roles reversed, with you the spy.

The lights go up. What glittering audience
    Tier above tier notices finally
Your ragged defeat, your jovial pretence?
    You stand still, but the bar is emptying fast.
Time to go home babe, though now you feel most
        tense.
    These games have little content. If you've lost
It doesn't matter tomorrow. Sleep well. Heaven knows
    Feverish people need more sleep than most
And need to learn all they can about repose.

THE EXPIRATION

So, so, breake off this last lamenting kisse,
  Which sucks two soules, and vapors Both away,
Turne thou ghost that way, and let mee turne this,
  And let our selves benight our happiest day,
We ask'd none leave to love; nor will we owe
  Any, so cheape a death, as saying, Goe;

Goe; and if that word have not quite kil'd thee,
  Ease mee with death, by bidding mee goe too.
Oh, if it have, let my word worke on mee,
  And a just office on a murderer doe.
Except it be too late, to kill me so,
  Being double dead, going, and bidding, goe.

JOHN DONNE (1572–1631)   257

THE DIVORCE

At first it was only an imperceptible quivering of
      the skin –
'As you wish' – where the flesh is darkest.
'What's wrong with you?' – Nothing. Milky dreams
of embraces; next morning, though,
the other looks different, strangely bony.
Razor-sharp misunderstanding. 'That time, in Rome –'
I never said that. A pause. And furious palpitations,
a sort of hatred, strange. 'That's not the point.'
Repetitions. Radiantly clear, this certainty:
From now on all is wrong. Odourless and sharp,
like a passport photo, this unknown person
with a glass of tea at table, with staring eyes.
It's no good, no good, no good:
litany in the head, a slight nausea.
End of reproaches. Slowly the whole room
Fills with guilt right up to the ceiling.
This complaining voice is strange, only not
the shoes that drop with a bang, not the shoes.
Next time, in an empty restaurant,
slow motion, bread crumbs, money is discussed,
laughing – The dessert tastes of metal.
Two untouchables. Shrill reasonableness.
'Not so bad really.' But at night
the thoughts of vengeance, the silent fight, anonymous

like two bony barristers, two large crabs
in water. Then the exhaustion. Slowly
the scab peels off. A new tobacconist,
a new address. Pariahs, horribly relieved.
Shades growing paler. These are the documents.
This is the bunch of keys. This is the scar.

HANS MAGNUS ENZENSBERGER (1929–   ),   259
TRANS. MICHAEL HAMBURGER

RETURN

Return often and take me,
beloved sensation, return and take me –
when the memory of the body awakens,
and old desire again runs through the blood;
when the lips and the skin remember,
and the hands feel as if they touch again.

Return often and take me at night,
when the lips and the skin remember . . .

C. P. CAVAFY (1863–1933),
     TRANS. RAE DALVEN

CAFÉ TRIESTE: SAN FRANCISCO
To L. G.

To this corner of Grant and Vallejo
I've returned like an echo
to the lips that preferred
then a kiss to a word.

Nothing has changed here. Neither
the furniture nor the weather.
Things, in one's absence, gain
permanence, stain by stain.

Cold, through the large steamed windows
I watch the gesturing weirdos,
the bloated breams that warm
up their aquarium.

Evolving backward, a river
becomes a tear, the real
becomes memory which
can, like fingertips, pinch

just the tail of a lizard
vanishing in the desert
which was eager to fix
a traveler with a sphinx.

Your golden mane! Your riddle!
The lilac skirt, the brittle
ankles! The perfect ear
rendering 'read' as 'dear.'

Under what cloud's pallor
now throbs the tricolor
of your future, your past
and present, swaying the mast?

Upon what linen waters
do you drift bravely toward
new shores, clutching your beads
to meet the savage needs?

Still, if sins are forgiven,
that is, if souls break even
with flesh elsewhere, this joint,
too, must be enjoyed

as afterlife's sweet parlor
where, in the clouded squalor,
saints and the ain'ts take five,
where I was first to arrive.

262   JOSEPH BRODSKY (1940–   )

VOYAGE TO CYTHERA

My heart, a seagull rocketed and spun
about the rigging, dipping joyfully;
our slow prow rocking under cloudless sky
was like an angel drunk with the live sun.

What's that out there? Those leagues of hovering
     sand?
'It's Cythera famous in the songs,
the gay old dogs' El Dorado, it belongs
to legend. Look closely, it's a poor land.'

Island of secret orgies none profess,
the august shade of Aphrodite plays
like clouds of incense over your blue bays,
and weights the heart with love and weariness.

Island whose myrtle esplanades arouse
our nerves, here heart-sighs and the adoration
of every land and age and generation
ramble like coal-red roses on a house

to the eternal cooing of the dove.
'No, Cythera crumbles, cakes and dries,
a rocky desert troubled by shrill cries . . .
And yet I see one portent stretch above

us. Is it a temple where the pagan powers
hover in naked majesty to bless
the arbours, gold-fish ponds and terraces;
and the young priestess is in love with flowers?

No, nosing through these shoals, and coming near
enough to scare the birds with our white sails,
we saw a man spread-eagled on the nails
of a cross hanging like a cypress there.

Ferocious vultures choking down thick blood
gutted the hanging man, already foul;
each smacked its beak like the flat of a trowel
into the private places of their food.

His eyes were holes and his important paunch
oozed lazy, looping innards down his hips;
those scavengers, licking sweetmeats from their lips,
had hung his pouch and penis on a branch.

Under his foot-soles, shoals of quadrupeds
with lifted muzzles nosed him round and guzzled;
a hugh antediluvian reptile muscled
through them like an executioner with his aides.

Native of Cythera, initiate,
how silently you hung and suffered insult
in retribution for your dirty cult
and orgasms only death could expiate.

Ridiculous hanged man, my sins confirm
your desecration; when I saw you seethe,
I felt my nausea mounting to my teeth,
the drying bile-stream of my wasted sperm.

Poor devil with sweet memories, your laws
are mine; before you, I too felt those jaws:
black panther, lancing crow, the Noah's Ark
that loved to chafe my flesh and leave their mark.

I'd lost my vision clinging to those shrouds,
I feared the matching blues of sky and sea;
all things were henceforth black with blood for me,
and plunged my heart in allegoric clouds ...

Nothing stands upright in your land, oh Lust,
except my double, hanging at full length –
Oh God, give me the courage and the strength
to see my heart and body without disgust.

CHARLES BAUDELAIRE (1821–1867),   265
TRANS. ROBERT LOWELL

LIGHT LISTENED

O what could be more nice
Than her ways with a man?
She kissed me more than twice
Once we were left alone.
Who'd look when he could feel?
She'd more sides than a seal.

The close air faintly stirred.
Light deepened to a bell,
The love-beat of a bird.
She kept her body still
And watched the weather flow.
We live by what we do.

All's known, all, all around:
The shape of things to be;
A green thing loves the green
And loves the living ground.
The deep shade gathers night;
She changed with changing light.

We met to leave again
The time we broke from time;
A cold air brought its rain,
The singing of a stem.
She sang a final song;
Light listened when she sang.

MEETING IN A LIFT

We stepped into the lift. The two of us, alone.
We looked at each other and that was all.
Two lives, a moment, fullness, bliss.
At the fifth floor she got out and I went on up
knowing I would never see her again,
that it was a meeting once and for all,
that if I followed her I would be like a dead man in her
    tracks
and that if she came back to me
it would only be from the other world.

VLADIMÍR HOLAN (1905–1980),
    TRANS. JARMILA AND IAN MIHER

DOING, A FILTHY PLEASURE IS, AND SHORT

Doing, a filthy pleasure is, and short;
And done, we straight repent us of the sport:
Let us not then rush blindly on unto it,
Like lustfull beasts, that onely know to doe it:
For lust will languish, and that heat decay,
But thus, thus, keeping endlesse Holy-day,
Let us together closely lie, and kisse,
There is no labour, nor so shame in this;
This hath pleas'd, doth please, and long will please;
     never
Can this decay, but is beginning ever.

PETRONIUS (1ST CENTURY AD),
TRANS. BEN JONSON

MY TIME'S TOO SHORT

Phaedra
My time's too short, your highness. It was I,
who lusted for your son with my hot eye.
The flames of Aphrodite maddened me;
I loathed myself, and yearned outrageously
like a starved wolf to fall upon the sheep.
I wished to hold him to me in my sleep
and dreamt I had him. Then Oenone's tears,
troubled my mind; she played upon my fears,
until her pleading forced me to declare
I loved your son. He scorned me. In despair,
I plotted with my nurse, and our conspiracy
made you believe your son assaulted me.
Oenone's punished; fleeing from my wrath,
she drowned herself, and found a too easy path
to death and hell. Perhaps you wonder why
I still survive her, and refuse to die?
Theseus, I stand before you to absolve
your noble son. Sire, only this resolve
upheld me, and made me throw down my knife.

I've chosen a slower way to end my life –
Medea's poison; chills already dart
along my boiling veins and squeeze my heart.
A cold composure I have never known
gives me a moment's poise. I stand alone
and seem to see my outraged husband fade
and waver into death's dissolving shade.
My eyes at last give up their light, and see
the day they've soiled resume its purity.

JEAN RACINE (1639–1699),
TRANS. ROBERT LOWELL

BEFORE PARTING

A month or twain to live on honeycomb
Is pleasant; but one tires of scented time,
Cold sweet recurrence of accepted rhyme,
And that strong purple under juice and foam
Where the wine's heart has burst;
Nor feel the latter kisses like the first.

Once yet, this poor one time; I will not pray
Even to change the bitterness of it,
The bitter taste ensuring on the sweet,
To make your tears fall where your soft hair lay
All blurred and heavy in some perfumed wise
Over my face and eyes.

And yet who knows what end the scythèd wheat
Makes of its foolish poppies' mouths of red?
These were not sown, these are not harvested,
They grow a month and are cast under feet
And none has care thereof,
As none has care of a divided love.

I know each shadow of your lips by rote,
Each change of love in eyelids and eyebrows;
The fashion of fair temples tremulous
With tender blood, and colour of your throat;
I know not how love is gone out of this,
Seeing that all was his.

Love's likeness there endures upon all these:
But out of these one shall not gather love.
Day hath not strength nor the night shade enough
To make love whole and fill his lips with ease,
As some bee-builded cell
Feels at filled lips the heavy honey swell.

I know not how this last month leaves your hair
Less full of purple colour and hid spice,
And that luxurious trouble of closed eyes
Is mixed with meaner shadow and waste care;
And love, kissed out by pleasure, seems not yet
Worth patience to regret.

A. C. SWINBURNE (1837–1909)

FINIS

Having sucked deep
In a sweet peony,
A bee creeps
Out of its hairy recesses.

BASHO (1644–1694), TRANS. NOBUYUKI YUASA

ACKNOWLEDGMENTS

Thanks are due to the following copyright holders for permission to reprint poems in this volume:

Aitken, Stone & Wylie Ltd. for Charles Baudelaire, tr. Roy Campbell, 'The Sisters'.

Anvil Press Poetry Ltd. for J. W. Von Goethe, tr. Michael Hamburger, 'Roman Elegy 1a'; Theodore Różewicz, tr. Adam Czerniawski, 'Draft for a Contemporary Love Poem'; Paul Verlaine, tr. Alistair Elliot 'A thousand and Three', 'Anointed Vessel'.

Bloodaxe Books Ltd. for Alistair Elliot's translations of Charles Baudelaire, 'The Giantess', 'She is not Satisfied', Pierre de Ronsard, 'Elegy XIX', José-Maria de Heredia; 'Antony and Cleopatra'.

University of California Press for Tristan Corbière, tr. C. F. MacIntyre, 'To the Eternal Feminine'.

Jonathan Clowes Ltd. for Kingsley Amis, 'Nothing to Fear'.

Doubleday and Co. Inc. for Theodore Roethke, 'Light Listened', 'The Partner', 'The Sensualists' 'The Dream', 'The Voice'.

Faber and Faber Inc. for Louis MacNeice, 'Meeting Point'; Thom Gunn, 'Carnal Knowledge'.

Farrar, Straus & Giroux, Inc. for Joseph Brodsky, 'Roman Elegies IV', 'Seven Strophes', 'Folk Tune',

'Café Trieste: San Francisco'; John Berryman, 'Ah when you drift . . .', 'Your Shining'; Thom Gunn, 'The Feel of Hands', 'Modes of Pleasure', 'The Bed', 'Fever'; Jean Racine, tr. Robert Lowell, 'My time's too short'; Randall Jarrell, 'In Nature there is neither Right nor Left nor Wrong'; Charles Baudelaire, tr. Robert Lowell, 'Voyage to Cythera'.

David R. Godine, Publisher, Inc. for Charles Baudelaire, tr. Richard Howard, 'Invitation to the Voyage', 'The Head of Hair'.

Michael Hamburger for his translation of Hans Magnus Enzenberger, 'The Divorce'.

Harcourt Brace & Company for Heinrich Heine, tr. Louis Untermeyer, 'The Morning After'.

HarperCollins Inc. for Yehuda Amichai, tr. Harold Schimmel, 'We Did It'; Sylvia Plath, 'Zoo Keeper's Wife'.

HarperCollins Publishers Ltd. for Vidyāpati, tr. Deben Bhattacharya, 'Twin Hills', 'New Love', 'Sad Love'.

Selima Hill for 'The Ram'.

Liveright for Hart Crane, 'National Winter Garden'.

Robert Maître for 'The Woman Underneath'.

James Michie for his translation of Catullus, 'Many think Quintia's beautiful'.

William Moebius for his translation of Philodemus, 'Hello there'.

John Murray (Publishers) Ltd. for John Betjeman, 'Late-flowering Lust'.

New Directions Publishing Corporation for Octavio
Paz, tr. Eliot Weinberger, 'Proof', 'Counterparts', 'Last
Dawn'; tr. Charles Tomlinson, 'Touch'; Dylan Thomas,
'On the Marriage of a Virgin'; Delmore Schwartz,
'Aria'; Denise Levertov, 'The Wife'.
Oxford University Press Inc. for Robert Graves, 'The
Quiet Glades of Eden', 'Gift of Sight', 'The Succubus',
'Down, Wanton, Down', 'The Naked and the Nude',
'Ulysses', 'The Metaphor', 'The Death Grapple'.
Oxford University Press Ltd. for Fleur Adcock, 'Note
on Propertius 1.5'; Anne Stevenson, 'Himalayan
Balsam'; Craig Raine, 'Sexual Couplets'.
Penguin USA for D. H. Lawrence, 'Figs', Pablo
Neruda, tr. W. S. Merwin, 'Girl lithe and tawny'.
Penguin Books Ltd. for Bhartṛhari, tr John Brough, 'If
the Forest of her Hair', 'Three Poems'; 'Breasts'.
Random House, Inc. for Robinson Jeffers, 'The Maid's
Thought'.
Rogers, Coleridge & White for C. P. Cavafy, tr. Rae
Dalven, 'One Night', 'Days of 1901', 'In Despair'.
George Sassoon for Siegfried Sassoon, 'Foot Inspection'.
Vernon Scannell for 'Act of Love'.

Every effort has been made to trace copyright holders
of material in this book. The publishers apologize if
any material has been included without permission and
would be glad to be told of anyone who has not been
consulted.

INDEX OF FIRST LINES

284